IN HEAVEN
WITH
THE HUNGRY MONK

A NEW BOOK OF SECRETS
by
Claire Burgess   Lucy Baldwin   Sue and Nigel Mackenzie
Drawings by Graham Jeffery

Hungry Monk Publications
The Old Coach House
Jevington Near Polegate
Sussex BN26 5QF
01323 483989 or 482178

First published in November 1997

This book is to mark the
30th Anniversary of
The Hungry Monk and is
dedicated to all our customers.

STARTERS

SOUPS

18th Century Gardeners Soup	1
Mussel, Potato and Rocket Soup	2
Yellow Pepper and Sage Soup	3
Broad Bean Soup with Crisp Bacon	4
Chilled Fresh Salmon Soup with Watercress Cream	5

FISH STARTERS

Tian of Smoked Salmon and Artichoke Hearts	6
Ceviche of Scallops	7
Creamy Squid and Prawn Risotto	8
Fresh Salmon Fishcake with Vermouth and Prawn Sauce	9
Smoked Salmon and Fresh Lobster with Saffron Sauce	11
Tartare of Fresh Tuna with Lemon Ratatouille	14
Blinis of Smoked Salmon	16

MEAT STARTERS

Duck and Potato Cake with Apple and Sage Sauce	17
Watercress Salad with Venison Sausages and Pickled Walnuts	18
Thai Beef with Cucumber, Waterchestnuts and Soy Sauce	19
Salad of Smoked Chicken, Prawns and Avocado on Tagliatelli	20
Ham and Mushrooms on Rosti	21

VEGETARIAN STARTERS

Celeriac, Quails Egg and Avocado Salad	23
Layered Italian Terrine	24
Goats Cheese and Pistachio Soufflé	26
Onion Tarte Tatin	28
Beetroot Mousse with Mange Tout	29
Salad of Rocket, Puy Lentils and Parmesan with Balsamic Shallots	31

MAIN COURSES

FISH

Seared Scallops with Pancetta and Sage on a Potato Cake	33
Sea Bream with Red Wine and Shallot Sauce	35
Cod with a Parsley and Garlic Crust and Sorrel Sauce	36
Salmon on Tagliolini with Ginger, Garlic and Coriander Sauce	37
Brochette of Monkfish, Scallops on Tagliatelli with Hollandaise	39
Croustade of Lobster and Spinach with Lemon Herb Butter	40
Fillet of Cod with Deep Fried Anchovies and Sweet Pepper Sauce	42
Fish Stew with Fennel and Pernod	44

LAMB

Lamb with a Tapenade Crust and Fennel and Cream Sauce	46
Lamb with Sweet Ratatouille	47
Lamb with Aubergine Puree and Garlic and Rosemary Sauce	48

PORK

Pan Fried Fillet of Pork with Black Pudding and Mustard Sauce	50
Fillet of Pork with Fragrant Rice and Thai Curry Sauce	51

GAME

Daube of Venison, Pheasant and Pigeon with Horseradish Dumplings	53
Pan Fried Guinea Fowl with Green Peppercorns and Shallots	55
Roast Quail with Raisin, Grape and Madeira Sauce	56
Rabbit Stifatho	58
Rabbit Roasted in Prosciutto with Bacon Sauce	59
Pan Fried Pigeon Breast Stuffed with Foie Gras	61
Partridge with Bacon and Marsala Sauce	63

CHICKEN

Chicken Normande	64

VEGETABLES

PUDDINGS

MISCELLANEOUS

18th CENTURY GARDENERS SOUP

This is a delicately flavoured soup which contains 5 different garden vegetables and is of course ideal for vegetarians.

To serve 4

2oz/50g butter
2 tablespoons of flour
1¾ pints/1 litre of vegetable stock
¼ pint/150ml cream
salt & freshly ground black pepper
2 tablespoons of chopped parsley

1 onion
4oz/100g carrots
4oz/100g leeks
4 spears of asparagus
4oz/100g swede

Preparation
Peel and finely chop the onions. Peel and thinly slice the carrots. Wash and finely chop the leeks. Remove the tips of the asparagus. Peel and cube the swede. Make the vegetable stock.

Method
Take a heavy-based pan and melt the butter, add the onions and cook until soft. Then stir in the flour to form a roux and follow this by pouring in the vegetable stock stirring all the time to make a smooth sauce. Cook this for about 20 minutes to reduce and then stir in the cream, seasoning to taste.

When you are ready to serve the soup, bring it gently to the boil and toss in the carrots followed by the swede. Three or four minutes later add the asparagus and the leeks. Continue to cook for another 1 or 2 minutes throwing in the parsley. Stir and serve.

MUSSEL, POTATO AND ROCKET SOUP

To serve 4

4lb/2kg live mussels
¼ pint/150ml of dry white wine   3floz/90ml vermouth
2 medium potatoes   ¼ pint/150ml cream
8oz/200g of rocket   2oz/50g butter
1 large onion   juice of one lemon
1¾ pints/1 l of vegetable stock   salt & freshly ground black pepper
(plus stock from the mussels)

Preparation
Peel and roughly chop the onions and potatoes. Remove the stalks from the
rocket and set aside, roughly chop the leaves. Wash and scrub the mussels
thoroughly under cold running water to remove and grit and barnacles,
discarding any that are open or cracked. Take a large heavy-based pan with
a tight fitting lid - tip in the white wine and mussels. Cover and steam for
about eight minutes until the shells have opened. Remove from the heat and
transfer the mussels and their liquor to a large bowl. Shell the mussels and
discard any that have not opened. Strain the liquor through a fine sieve and
reserve.

Method
Take a large heavy-based saucepan and melt the butter. Add the potato,
onion and rocket stalks, cooking until the onions are soft. Pour in the
vegetable stock and bring to the boil. Continue to simmer until the potato is
soft. Now pour all this, along with the cream, into a food processor and
whiz until smooth before passing the soup through a strainer back into a
clean saucepan. Return this to the heat and tip in the mussels with their
liquor, the rocket leaves, vermouth and lemon juice. Continue to cook for a
few moments, adjust the seasoning and serve.

YELLOW PEPPER AND SAGE SOUP

To serve 4

6 yellow peppers	2 cloves of garlic
1 onion	2 pints/1 litre vegetable stock
3 sticks of celery	a little olive oil
1 bulb of fennel	¼ pint/150ml of cream
1 small green chilli	salt & freshly ground black pepper
2 tablespoons of chopped sage	parmesan shavings

Preparation

Wash and chop the celery and fennel. De-seed and finely chop the chilli.
Chop the onion. De-seed and dice the pepper into one-inch squares. Crush
the garlic.

Method

Heat the olive oil in a heavy-based pan and add the garlic, sage, onion,
celery, fennel, chilli and yellow peppers. Stir over a high heat until the
vegetables soften. Just cover the vegetables with stock and bring to the boil.
Simmer for 25 to 30 minutes until the vegetables are cooked. Whiz in a
food processor and pass through a sieve into a clean pan. At this point, you
may need to add a little more vegetable stock to thin the soup down. Add
the cream and season to taste.

Serve in warm bowls with the parmesan shavings on top.

BROAD BEAN SOUP WITH CRISP BACON

This is one of our most successful introductions of recent years- a surprisingly nice way of eating broad beans.

To serve 4

1lb/0.5kg shelled weight of fresh or frozen broad beans
1 onion
2 sticks of celery
1 medium potato
1¾ pints/1 litre vegetable stock
¼ pint/150ml double cream
2oz/50g butter
2floz/60ml of dry sherry
4 rashers of bacon

Preparation
Peel and chop the potato and the onions. Shell the broad beans. Wash and chop the celery sticks. Make the vegetable stock.

Method
Melt the butter in a heavy-based saucepan and fry the potato, onions and celery. After two or three minutes pour in the vegetable stock and bring to the boil. Toss in half the broad beans and continue to cook for about 25 minutes. Now pour in the cream and the rest of the broad beans and cook for 15 minutes more before transferring the whole mix into a food processor and whizzing until smooth. All this needs to be passed through a sieve into a clean saucepan where the seasoning should be adjusted. At this point, add the sherry.

Grill the bacon until crisp and serve in thin strips floating on the surface of the soup.

CHILLED FRESH SALMON SOUP WITH WATERCRESS CREAM

A very pretty looking soup with a dollop of watercress cream floating in the middle.

To serve 4

12oz/300g fresh salmon fillet
1 medium onion
1¾ pints/1 litre of vegetable stock
6 tomatoes
3floz/90ml vermouth
2oz/50g butter
¼ pint/150ml cream
juice of 1 lemon
salt and freshly ground black pepper

1 bunch of watercress
½ pint/300ml sour cream

Preparation
Peel and chop the onions. Roughly chop the tomatoes. Make the vegetable stock. Check the salmon for bones and cut into cubes. Remove the stalks from the watercress and discard. Then roughly chop the watercress leaves by hand.

Method
Melt the butter in a heavy-based pan and toss in the onions and tomatoes cooking for a few minutes. Pour in the vegetable stock and vermouth - bring to the boil and simmer for 5 minutes. Now tip in the cubes of salmon and season with salt and pepper. The idea is that we should now poach the salmon in the stock for 5 or 6 minutes until it is cooked before pouring in the cream and lemon juice. All that remains is to pour this mixture into a food processor and whiz to a soup like consistency before transferring into a clean bowl and chilling in the fridge.

To serve the soup first fold the chopped watercress into the sour cream and then season. Spoon the soup into the bowls and float a dollop of the sour cream mixture on top.

TIAN OF SMOKED SALMON AND ARTICHOKE HEARTS

Smoked salmon and thinly sliced cold artichoke hearts layered one on top of the other and coated with warm hollandaise.

To serve 4

8oz/200g sliced smoked salmon	**hollandaise - see page 27**
4 globe artichokes	**cayenne pepper**
2 lemons quartered	**fresh dill**

Preparation
The main task is to prepare the artichokes. To do this, put the lemon into a large saucepan of salted water and bring to the boil. Whilst this is happening, remove the stalks from the artichokes followed by the leaves and then scoop out the choke with a spoon. Place the hearts into the water together with the lemon and cook for about 20 minutes or until you are able to push a knife smoothly into the heart. You may wonder why the lemon has to be in the water - this is to stop the heart going black. Transfer the hearts into a colander and leave under a running cold tap for a minute or two to allow them to refresh. Drain and pat dry.

Method
The idea is to make a little tower or cairn in the middle of each plate alternating a slice of artichoke heart with a doubled over slice of smoked salmon. Try and keep your best looking slices of artichoke for the tops. Now is the moment to make the hollandaise, which should be poured hot over the tian just before serving. The whole works should be decorated with a sprinkling of cayenne pepper and a sprig of dill.

CEVICHE OF SCALLOPS

Scallops marinated in fresh lime juice and served uncooked.

To serve 4

8 large king scallops	selection of salad leaves
juice of 3 limes	french dressing
¼ pint/150ml olive oil	fresh dill
salt & freshly ground black pepper	

Preparation
All this should be done the day before serving. Clean and trim the scallops and slice them sideways (if they are large enough). Squeeze all the juice out of the limes into a bowl and add the olive oil and salt. Add a grind of black pepper and immerse the scallops. Transfer to the fridge and leave overnight where the effect of the lime juice will be to virtually cook the scallops whilst leaving them beautifully succulent and fresh tasting.

Method
The main task here is to present the ceviche in an attractive manner. Make a salad with different coloured leaves, getting as much height as you can and then arrange the scallops on top with a sprig of dill.

CREAMY SQUID AND PRAWN RISOTTO

To serve 4

3 medium squid	3floz/90ml vermouth
8 tiger prawns	4oz of grated parmesan cheese
8oz/200g risotto rice (aborio)	2floz/60ml double cream
1 medium onion	juice of one lemon
5oz/125g butter	salt & freshly ground black pepper
2 tablespoons of oil	2 tablespoons of chopped parsley
1½ pint/900ml vegetable stock	to serve - fresh parmesan shards

Preparation
Peel and chop the onion. Make the vegetable stock. Chop the parsley.
Prepare the squid by cleaning them, taking any skin off and slicing them
into thin strips. Shell the prawns. Mix the vegetable stock and vermouth
together.

Method
Take a large heavy-based saucepan and combine the butter and the oil,
when hot, tip in the onion and cook until soft. Pour in the risotto rice and
cook for one minute. Now, stirring gradually, add the vegetable stock a
ladle-full at a time until all has been absorbed by the rice. This is a time
consuming and rather boring process but resist the temptation to pour all the
stock in and walk away as this will produce a pudding like lump of rice that
is not what we want.

The time has now arrived when we can stir in the squid and prawns
followed shortly by the lemon juice, chopped parsley and cream. Season to
taste and finally stir in the grated parmesan. Serve with shards of fresh
parmesan on the top, using a potato peeler drawn across a block of cheese.

FRESH SALMON FISHCAKE WITH VERMOUTH AND PRAWN SAUCE

This is almost the most popular starter we do at The Hungry Monk- apart from being an excellent starter they make a delicious supper dish on their own with a little green salad.

To serve 4

8oz/200g salmon fillet	tabasco sauce
4oz/100g breadcrumbs	**juice of one lemon**
3 medium old potatoes	**4 sprigs of dill**
6oz/150g new potatoes	**2 egg yolks**
2 tablespoons of cream	**salt and freshly ground black pepper**
a little oil	

SAUCE
3floz/90ml vermouth
6oz/150g peeled prawns
½ pint/300ml cream
2 shallots
juice of one lemon
salt and freshly ground black pepper

Preparation
Cut the salmon fillets into small pieces. Peel and boil the old potatoes. Boil the new potatoes and dice them once cool. Separate the eggs. Chop the dill. Peel and chop the shallots for the sauce.

Method
Drain and mash the old potatoes with the cream until absolutely smooth. Now take a large bowl and combine the mashed potato with the raw salmon, new potato, the black pepper, salt, tabasco, lemon juice, dill, egg yolks and mustard.

Mix thoroughly. The next stage is the rather pleasurable business of forming the mixture into fishcakes. These should be approximately 3 inches across by 1 inch deep and should be liberally coated with the breadcrumbs. Place in the fridge and allow to rest for half an hour or so.

9

Whilst they are relaxing in the fridge you can turn your attention to the vermouth sauce. This should be made by taking a medium sized saucepan, pouring in the vermouth and heating with the shallots and lemon juice, reducing down as you do so. Then stir in the cream, adjust the seasoning and put to one side. Do not put the prawns in yet.

When you are ready to serve your fishcakes take them out of the fridge and put them into a pan of hot oil and fry for about 3 minutes each side until crisp. At the same time put the sauce back on the heat. Finally toss the prawns into the sauce and serve with the fishcakes decorated with a wedge of lemon and a sprig of parsley.

SMOKED SALMON AND FRESH LOBSTER WITH SAFFRON SAUCE

This is a lovely starter, very pretty looking as the lobster is entirely wrapped in smoked salmon and surrounded by a very attractive sauce.

To serve 4

4 slices of smoked salmon
1 medium sized cooked lobster
5floz/150ml double cream
salt and freshly ground black pepper
juice and zest of 1 lemon

DECORATION
black caviar
chervil

SAFFRON SAUCE
6 strands of saffron
2 shallots
3floz/90ml vermouth
5floz/150ml double cream
juice of one lemon
salt
freshly ground black pepper

SPECIAL EQUIPMENT
4 oval ramekins (~3" long)

Preparation
Lightly oil the ramekins. Remove the shell from the lobster - reserve the tail and claw meat in a cool place. Remove the zest from the lemon and squeeze the juice into a jug. Peel and chop the shallots for the sauce.

Method
The order of events is as follows - we are going to line the ramekins with smoked salmon and then take most of the lobster and put it through a food processor to make it into a cream. We then dollop this into the ramekins with a piece of really beautiful lobster meat set in the middle of each.

Therefore, the first task is to cut four good slices of lobster from the tail sections that you have been keeping in the fridge. Next, take the remaining lobster and put that in a food processor with the lemon juice, zest, salt and pepper. Bring to a smooth paste before pouring in all the cream, and re-starting the food processor. Now we have to be careful as we want the cream to gradually whip with the lobster to a reasonably thick consistency without going too far and having the cream split. We want something that is the consistency of heavy thick whipped cream. Spoon some of this mixture into the bottom of each ramekin onto the smoked salmon and place the piece of tail you cut earlier in the middle before spooning the rest of the mixture on top. Now fold over the smoked salmon and cover each with cling film. These can now be placed in the fridge and allowed to chill thoroughly and slightly set.

We now turn our attention to the sauce. This should be made well in advance, as it must be cold when it is served. Fry the shallots in the oil until soft. Then pour in the vermouth, saffron and lemon juice and reduce a little. Now pour in the double cream and season, then reduce still further. Pour into a jug and keep in the fridge.

To serve this dish turn the ramekins out onto the plate so that the folded smoked salmon is on the underside and surround with the saffron sauce. Finish with a sprinkling of mock caviar on the top and the chervil.

TARTARE OF FRESH TUNA WITH LEMON RATATOUILLE

To serve 4

8oz/200g fresh tuna fillet
juice of one lemon
freshly ground black pepper

RATATOUILLE

2 courgettes	**zest of one lemon**
1 small aubergine	**a tin of chopped tomatoes**
1 medium red pepper	**a sprig of fresh rosemary**
1 medium green pepper	**1 dessertspoon of sugar**
1 onion	**2 tablespoons of olive oil**
2 cloves of garlic	**salt and freshly ground black pepper**

EQUIPMENT
4 x tin ring moulds – 3½ x 1½ inches or 85mm x 40mm

Preparation
Peel and finely chop the onion and the garlic. Finely chop the courgette and aubergine. De-seed the red and green peppers and finely chop. Open the tin of chopped tomatoes.

Method
Heat the oil in a heavy based saucepan and tip in the onion, garlic, aubergine, courgette, red and green peppers and fry until soft. Follow this by tipping in the tomatoes, sugar, lemon zest, sprig of rosemary and seasoning. Continue to cook with a sheet of greaseproof paper over the surface of the ratatouille for 30 minutes on a low heat. While this is cooking you can carve slices of tuna through the fish at an angle rather as if you were carving smoked salmon. Returning to the ratatouille this can now be decanted into a bowl and placed in the fridge to cool thoroughly. We now have a bowl of ratatouille and some slices of raw tuna.

To finish the dish, place a tin ring mould in the middle of each plate and spread the ratatouille mixture to a depth of about half an inch across the bottom. Now take slices of the raw tuna and arrange on the top in each ring.

Follow this by a good squeeze of lemon juice, a grind of black pepper and turn on the grill to full heat.

When you are ready to serve the dish, flash each plate under the grill just long enough to sear the top of the fish while leaving its underside raw and the ratatouille beneath that, cold. Remove the ring and serve. For various reasons, it may not be possible for you to flash the tartare under the grill whilst it is on the plate that you are going to serve it on. In this case, you can assemble the ring moulds with their contents on a non-stick-baking tray suitable in size to fit under your grill. Great care will have to be taken when you transfer these onto the plates and a broad slice will have to be employed if you are not going to see the ratatouille drop away.

BLINIS OF SMOKED SALMON

A small thick pancake with an arrangement of smoked salmon and creme fraiche on the top.

To serve 4

BLINI MIX	10oz/250g smoked salmon
1 egg	7floz/200ml creme fraiche
½ pint/300ml of milk	tabasco sauce
1 heaped teaspoon of yeast	juice of one lemon
1 teaspoon of sugar	dill
8oz/200g of flour	salt & freshly ground black pepper
1 teaspoon of salt	prawns & salmon eggs to decorate

Preparation

Warm the milk until it is at blood heat. Mix the sugar and yeast together in a small bowl and pour over the warm milk. Now whisk in the eggs followed by the flour and the salt. When all is dissolved and smooth, leave to stand in a warm place for thirty minutes. Slice the smoked salmon into thin strips and chop the dill.

Method

The first thing is to make the four blinis. This is not difficult - simply take a small non-stick frying pan and pour in a little oil raising the heat to a medium level. Pour a generous spoonful of the batter into the middle of the pan and it will spread just so far and no more, gently bubbling. After a minute or so, turn the blini and cook the other side. Because of the yeast in the mixture, it should start to rise at this stage and turn a golden brown. Do not over-cook - the whole process should take little more than a minute and a half. Lift each blini out of the pan and onto some kitchen tissue to drain. To serve this dish, you can either eat the blinis now whilst still warm or put them in the fridge and eat them cold later (warm is slightly nicer).

The next task is to mix the creme fraiche with the lemon juice, tabasco and dill followed by the ground black pepper. Add the smoked salmon and only then check for saltiness. The mixture is now ready to be dolloped in to the middle of each blini and decorated with prawns and salmon eggs.

DUCK AND POTATO CAKE WITH APPLE AND SAGE SAUCE

This is the ducky brother of fishcakes - we call them *Quakes*!
To serve 4

4 duck legs
6oz/150g of new potatoes
3 medium old potatoes
2 tablespoons of double cream
4 spring onions
2 egg yolks
salt and freshly ground black pepper
4oz/100g of fresh breadcrumbs

FOR THE SAUCE
6 apples
¼ pint/150ml cider
2oz/50g sugar
3floz/90ml cream
6 chopped sage leaves

Preparation

Start by roasting the duck legs, which you should have seasoned with salt
and pepper, for about an hour in a baking dish at gas mark 6/200°C. Whilst
this is going on, boil and dice the new potatoes. Peel, boil and mash the old
potatoes with the cream and some salt and pepper. Trim and chop the spring
onions and make some fresh breadcrumbs in a food processor. Peel and
chop the apples and chop the sage for the sauce.

Method

Because the duck legs are going to take about an hour to cook, you should
have time to make the sauce before making the duck cakes. This is simply
done by cooking the apples, cider and sugar together with salt and black
pepper and pureeing in a food processor. Pour back into the saucepan and
stir in the cream and fresh sage. That's all there is to it.

Now to the duck cakes. Take the meat off the duck legs and roughly chop.
Put in to a large bowl and tip in the new potatoes, the mashed potatoes, the
spring onions and the eggs. Thoroughly mix all this before adjusting the
seasoning with the salt and pepper. Now shape the mixture into something
similar to a fish cake - about 3 inches across and one inch high - and
liberally coat with the breadcrumbs. Put the duck cakes on a tray and chill
in the fridge for half and hour or so or until you are ready to serve them.
Finally, heat some oil in the pan and fry them for three or four minutes each
side until crisp, golden and utterly appetising to look at. Serve with the
apple and sage sauce.

WATERCRESS SALAD WITH VENISON SAUSAGES AND PICKLED WALNUTS

Though warm salads have slightly gone out of fashion, this is still too delicious to leave out of the book.

To serve 4

4 venison sausages
8 pickled walnuts
1 large bunch of watercress
1 radicchio lettuce
salt & freshly ground black pepper
a little oil

WARM VINAIGRETTE
4 tablespoons of vinegar
from the walnuts
1 tablespoon redcurrant jelly
1 teaspoon english mustard
3floz/90ml red wine

Preparation
Fry venison sausages in a little oil until cooked. Transfer onto some kitchen paper and allow to cool. Cut diagonal slices approximately one quarter of an inch thick and set to one side. Wash and trim the watercress. Cut the pickled walnuts into quarter inch slices.

Method
Arrange four salads using the radichio to form an outer ring and then fill the centre with watercress. Take a frying pan of heated oil and toss in the slices of venison sausage. Cook them until they begin to go golden and then pour in the other ingredients - the vinegar from the walnuts, the redcurrant jelly, the English mustard, red wine, salt and pepper and finally, just before serving, the pickled walnuts. All that now remains is to put an equal amount of this delicious mixture on to the top of each salad.

THAI BEEF WITH CUCUMBER, WATERCHESTNUTS AND SOY SAUCE

Good meat starters are fairly few and far between - this continues to be the most popular meat starter that we do at the Hungry Monk and is particularly good if one is having fish as a main course.

To serve 4

12oz/300g of beef fillet
1 red pepper
1 yellow pepper
1 small tin of waterchestnuts
6 spring onions
¼ of a cucumber
a little oil

SERVE WITH
fresh coriander leaves

THE MARINADE
¼ pint/150ml dry white wine
1 inch/25mm root ginger
2 cloves of garlic
teaspoon of five spice
3 tablespoons of soy sauce
1 tablespoon of dijon mustard
1 tablespoon of clear honey
2 tablespoons of white wine vinegar
6 shakes of tabasco
ground black pepper

Preparation
Cut the fillet steak into half-inch thick slices. Then cut the slices into half-inch thick strips. De-seed and chop the red and yellow peppers into strips. Trim and chop the spring onions. Chop the waterchestnuts. Cut the cucumber into half-inch batons. Make the marinade by combining all the ingredients and whizzing in the food processor for a minute or so.

Method
Take the wok and pour in the oil raising to a fairly high heat. Toss in the strips of fillet steak and vegetables, vigorously shaking the wok so that the beef is quickly sealed on all sides. Then pour in the marinade and continue to cook for about another two minutes depending on how well you like your beef to be done. Finally, serve this mixture in small warmed bowls if it is a starter, or with soft noodles if it is for a supper dish or main course. Decorate with coriander.

SALAD OF SMOKED CHICKEN PRAWNS AND AVOCADO ON TAGLIATELLI

To serve 4

2 smoked chicken breasts
8 cooked king prawns
1 avocado pear
3 tablespoons horseradish sauce
1 dessertspoon english mustard
2 tablespoons balsamic vinegar
¼ pint/150ml of olive oil
3floz/90ml double cream
juice of one lemon

salt and freshly ground black pepper
3 sprigs of coriander
small packet of fresh tagliatelli
1 tablespoon of olive oil
salt

Preparation
Take a large pan of salted water. Add a tablespoon of olive oil and bring to the boil. Toss in the tagliatelli and cook for 5 to 8 minutes until the pasta is al dente. Drain and refresh in a colander under a cold running tap. Drain again and set aside.

Cut the smoked chicken into slices. Remove the shells from the cooked prawns.

Method
Start by making the dressing in a small bowl by combining the horseradish sauce, English mustard and balsamic vinegar. Next, gently whisk in the olive oil followed by the double cream. Season and finish by stirring in the lemon juice. The next task is to peel, stone and chop the avocados.

How you present this dish is very much a matter of taste. You can put the pasta on the plate first having first tossed it in the horseradish dressing and then arrange the avocado, chicken slices and king prawns on the top, decorating with a few leaves of coriander. If you do it this way, remember that the avocado will go black and so this can only be done shortly before serving. Our own personal preference is to toss all the ingredients together in a large bowl.

HAM AND MUSHROOMS ON ROSTI

Rosti is one of those things everybody loves - adding ham and mushrooms just makes it even more delicious.

To serve 4

8oz/200g ham	**SAUCE**
5oz/125g button mushrooms	**2oz/50g butter**
5oz/125g oyster mushrooms	**1 tablespoon of flour**
3 large old potatoes	**¾ pint/450ml milk**
1 medium onion	**3floz/90ml sherry**
salt & freshly ground black pepper	**3floz/90ml double cream**
oil	**1 sprig of thyme**

SPECIAL EQUIPMENT
Yorkshire pudding tray or similar with 4 x 4 inch diameter moulds

Preparation and Method
Peel the potatoes and place in a colander over a large saucepan of boiling water. Steam for 10 minutes with the lid on. Turn off the heat and allow to stand. What you are looking for is a situation where the outside of the potato is soft enough for a knife to penetrate, but the interior is still quite raw. Any more cooked than this and it just won't grate. We would recommend that you do all this the day before you are going to serve the dish. Peel and finely chop the onions.

The following day - slice the mushrooms and cut the ham into half-inch slices and cut again into strips for the sauce. Using a grater with large slots, grate the potato into a bowl for the rosti. Pre heat the oven to gas mark 6/200°C. Take a large sauté pan and heat the oil. Fry the onions until soft and tip them into the bowl of grated potato and season. Do not put the frying pan away as we are now going to fry the mushrooms in a little oil and set them to one side. We now want to make the sauce. We do this by making a roux with the butter and flour in a heavy-based pan and pouring in the milk. Finish by pouring in the sherry and adjusting the seasoning. Tip in the ham and the mushrooms and the thyme. Stir gently before finishing with the cream.

The final task is to make the rosti. This is done by putting a little oil into each mould in the tart tin and putting in to the oven for 1 or 2 minutes to allow it to heat up. Take out of the oven and spoon enough of the grated potato into each mould for it to form a thin loose layer. Now return to the middle of the oven for 10 to 12 minutes until golden brown and crisp. When they are ready, remove from the oven and allow to cool before transferring them with a slice to a piece of kitchen tissue to drain. Keep warm and serve with generous spoonfuls of the ham and mushroom sauce poured half over the rosti. Don't forget to remove the sprig of thyme from the sauce!

CELERIAC, QUAILS EGG AND AVOCADO SALAD

To serve 4

1 celeriac
juice of one lemon
2oz/50g raisins
2 red apples
2oz/50g walnuts
2 tablespoons of chopped parsley
salt & freshly ground black pepper
8 quails eggs
1 avocado pear

LEMON MAYONNAISE
1 egg yolk
1 teaspoon of mustard
juice of one lemon
½pint/300ml olive oil

Preparation

Peel and grate the celeriac immediately mixing with the lemon juice to prevent it going black. Add salt and pepper. Core and chop the apples. Roughly chop the walnuts. Boil the quails eggs for 3 minutes and cool under cold running water before taking off the shells.

Method

We will start by making the lemon mayonnaise which is much easier than it sounds. Put the egg yolks, mustard and lemon juice together in a bowl. Whisk together and pour on the olive oil in a steady stream whisking all the time. This recipe is for a thin mayonnaise. Therefore, do not expect it to become that thick. A word of warning - it is important for all the ingredients to be at the same temperature - not cold but room temperature.

To assemble this delicious starter, simply combine the celeriac with the raisins, apples, walnuts and chopped parsley. Then tip in the lemon mayonnaise and combine all the ingredients thoroughly. Position a little dome-like pile of this mixture in the middle of each plate and finish by decorating with slices of avocado pear and 3 half quail eggs on the very top. Decorate with a sprig of flat leaf parsley.

LAYERED ITALIAN TERRINE

A delicious construction of layers of Mediterranean vegetables interleaved with goats cheese and pesto on toast and held together with lots of olive oil in a long terrine.

To serve 4

2 medium sized aubergines
1 red, yellow and green pepper
3 courgettes
4 tomatoes
9oz/225g spinach
6 slices of white bread
6oz/150g goats cheese
¼ pint/150ml olive oil
pesto see page 103

EQUIPMENT
1 rectangular terrine

Preparation
Start with the aubergines. These need to be topped and tailed and then cut longways from top to bottom in quarter inch thick slices. Lay on a plate and sprinkle with salt and leave to sweat for half an hour. Once you have done this rinse off the salt and pat dry.

The red, green and yellow peppers need to be de-seeded and chopped into quarters. Cut the courgettes longways into quarter inch thick slices. Cut the tomatoes through the width of the fruit again into quarter inch thick slices. Wash cook and drain the spinach and squeeze it dry in a clean tea towel. Cut and toast the slices of bread and remove the crusts. Cut the goats cheese into slices. Make the pesto (see page 103). Line the terrine with bakewell paper. Preheat the oven to gas mark 7/220°C.

Method
Lay the peppers skin side down on a flat baking tray, brush them with olive oil and sprinkle with pepper and salt. Put in the oven for about 15 minutes until the skin begins to blister. Remove and allow to cool.

The aubergines need to be fried in olive oil until they are golden both sides as do the courgettes. Season both the aubergines and courgettes well and save the oil from the pan. Remove the skins from the peppers, this is more easily done when they are still warm.

Now starts the really fun bit - assembling the terrine. We start by spreading pesto on the toast and putting a layer on the bottom of the terrine - pesto upward. Then lay slices of aubergines, tomatoes, spinach, courgettes, peppers and a layer of goat's cheese before putting the second piece of pesto toast in place. Then repeat another round of the vegetables again ending with goat's cheese, before topping the whole thing with the third layer of toast only this time with the pesto facing downwards. Now pour over that oil you kept from the pan and fold over the greaseproof paper.

For the terrine to be a success it has to be pressed well down. This probably means you are going to have to cut a piece of thin wood that fits just inside your terrine, this allows you to put heavy weights onto the top of the terrine and transfer the whole shooting match into the fridge. Let the terrine stand for 24 hours or so to allow it to set.

When you are ready to serve you can turn the terrine out onto a plate - something that can be easily done with the aid of the greaseproof paper. The terrine should be cut with a very sharp knife into thick slices, then served with a little salad of rocket and buckets of French dressing.

GOATS CHEESE AND PISTACHIO SOUFFLE

An easy to cook double baked soufflé.

To serve 4

3oz/75g goats cheese
1oz/25g butter
1 tablespoon of flour
5 tablespoons of milk
1 egg yolk
4 egg whites
salt and freshly ground black pepper

TO COAT RAMEKINS
2 tablespoons pistachio nuts
1 tablespoon bread crumbs
1 tablespoon parmesan
a little butter
3oz/75g cubed goat's cheese

Preparation
Separate the eggs keeping one yolk and the four whites. Heat the oven to gas mark 5/190°C. Toast the pistachio nuts on a baking tray until they are golden- it should only take about 4 or 5 minutes. Take 3oz-75g of the goat's cheese and slice up into cubes and crumble the rest of the cheese into a bowl. Butter the insides of the ramekins. Cut a greaseproof paper ring to fit exactly in the bottom of each of the ramekins. Put the roasted pistachio nuts into the food processor with the breadcrumbs and the parmesan and whiz until everything is a similar consistency. Now shake this breadcrumb mixture into the ramekins and allow as much as possible to stick to the sides before shaking off the excess. Put the ramekins in the fridge to chill. Reserve the remaining breadcrumb mixture.

Method
Start by putting a kettle on to boil, as you will need hot water later. Now make a goats cheese cream sauce by melting the butter in a heavy based pan, tipping in the flour, stirring to a roux then pouring in the milk to make into a cream sauce. Finish with the egg yolk and the crumbled goats cheese. Season to taste with the salt and pepper and put aside to cool.

This gives you an opportunity to beat the egg whites into stiff peaks and then fold about a quarter of the egg whites into the cheese sauce. This has the effect of slackening things a bit and makes it easier for you then to fold the rest of the egg whites into the sauce. At this stage, we have to move smartly, as the egg whites will not remain aerated forever. Take the ramekins out of the fridge and put the cubes of goat's cheese in the bottom.

Pour over the cheese sauce right up to the top and then sprinkle over the remaining breadcrumb mixture.

In order for the soufflés to rise evenly its a good idea at this stage to go round the top edge of each ramekin with a knife penetrating no more than quarter of an inch from the top surface. Now take an ordinary roasting tin and stand the four ramekins in it. Pour the boiling water from the kettle around the ramekins until you have a depth of approximately half the height of the ramekin, and place this bain marie into the middle of the preheated oven.

Cook for between 12 and 15 minutes during which time the soufflés should rise approximately half an inch above the top of the ramekins. Resist the temptation to open the oven door every few minutes, as they will never rise if you do.

When the soufflés are cooked we want to take them out of the oven. Allow them to cool sufficiently for you to be able to touch them. Then taking a flat baking tray, lifting each ramekin in turn, tip it out into the palm of your hand. Remove the greaseproof paper from the bottoms and then position the soufflés onto the baking tray with their tops uppermost again. The tray can now be put into the fridge and left until you are ready to serve them. At this point you simply put them back into an oven at gas mark 5 (190°C) for 5 minutes or so to warm them through.

Serve them on a bed of lamb's lettuce with French dressing.

ONION TARTE TATIN

Caramelised onions on a pastry base.

To Serve 4

1 pack of puff pastry	**TO SERVE**
4 large spanish onions	**green salad**
4oz/100g of sugar	**french dressing**
8floz/230ml balsamic vinegar	
2 tablespoons of olive oil	

Preparation
Peel and slice the onions. Take the puff pastry out of the freezer and allow to thaw. Preheat the oven to gas mark 6/200°C.

Method
This dish is started on the hob and finished in the oven. Therefore, we need a frying pan that is oven proof. To make the tart we are going to cover the pan with puff pastry. Roll out a piece of puff pastry approximately a quarter of an inch thick and large enough to cover the pan that you are using. Set to one side.

Pour the olive oil into the pan and cook the onions until they start turning a nice golden colour. At this stage, you can add the sugar and the salt and pepper and continue to cook until the sugar starts to caramelise. Now pour in the balsamic vinegar and continue to cook until things have reduced to a point where the juice is syrupy. At this stage, remove the pan from the heat and allow to cool before laying the pastry over the top of everything and trimming to shape. Now tuck the pastry well down inside the walls of the pan and make a hole in the middle of the pastry to let out the steam.

Transfer the whole thing to the oven where it is baked for about 20 minutes until the pastry is golden and cooked. Remove from the oven taking care not to burn your hands by grasping the handle - an easy mistake to make. Allow to cool thoroughly before putting a plate upside-down on the top of the pie and inverting the whole lot, so that the contents of the pan drop onto the plate, pastry first, with the onions now uppermost. Lift away the pan and you are now looking at your onion tarte tatin. All that remains is to cut it into thick slices and serve just warm with a green salad.

BEETROOT MOUSSE WITH MANGE TOUT

Curiously, while people don't seem to like beetroot, they love beetroot mousse - it looks a wonderful colour and it makes a very attractive starter.

To serve 4

8oz/200g of cooked and peeled beetroot
2 tablespoons of raspberry vinegar
2 egg whites
1 leaf of gelatine
¼ pint/150ml of double cream
2 tablespoons of dry sherry
salt & freshly ground black pepper

SERVE WITH
8oz/200g mange tout
french dressing

EQUIPMENT
4 x dariole moulds

Preparation
The beetroot mousse needs to be made at least 5 hours before you are going to eat it. Separate the eggs, keeping the whites. Soak the leaf gelatine in cold water. Top and tail the mange tout and cook them in salted boiling water for no more than a minute before draining them and refreshing under cold running water. Place them in the fridge. Lightly oil the dariole moulds.

Method
We start with the food processor into which we put the beetroot with the raspberry vinegar, salt and pepper. Whiz until smooth and pureed. Now heat the sherry in a little pan and take the gelatine that has been soaking in water, drain and slip it into the heated sherry to dissolve. Remove from the heat and allow the gelatine to dissolve. Now we can pour the sherry mixture into the food processor and giving it a whiz before pouring in the cream and whizzing again. The next task is to beat the egg whites to soft peaks in a separate bowl. Now take your beetroot mixture and fold it into the egg whites, trying to loose as little of the air and lightness as possible. Decant the mixture into your waiting dariole moulds and place in the fridge to chill thoroughly.

When the time comes to serve them, run the sides of the dariole moulds under a hot tap as this will help to release the beetroot mixture and give nice smooth shiny sides to the mousse. Each mousse should be put on a plate and surrounded by the mange tout and a generous dribbling of French dressing.

29

SALAD OF ROCKET, PUY LENTILS AND PARMESAN WITH BALSAMIC SHALLOTS

To serve 4

16 shallots
4oz/100g sugar
¼ pint/150ml balsamic vinegar
¼ pint/150ml red wine
1 sprig of rosemary
salt & freshly ground black pepper
3oz/75g puy lentils

Preparation
The only preparation for this is the balsamic shallots that really have to be made 2 or 3 days before you are going to make the salad. These are easily prepared. Simply peel the shallots and place in the pan together with the sugar, balsamic vinegar, red wine, rosemary, salt and pepper. Cook for about 20 minutes until the shallots are just soft to the point of a sharp knife. Allow to cool and transfer the shallots, with their juice, into a sterilised jam jar where they can live indefinitely.

Method
On the day that you are going to eat the salad, start by cooking the puy lentils with a pinch of salt in boiling water for about 35 minutes. Drain and allow them to go quite cold. Wash and trim the rocket.

To assemble the salad start by arranging the rocket on the plate. Then put a spoonful of puy lentils in the middle. Dress with French dressing. Now position the balsamic shallots with a spoonful of the balsamic vinegar they have been standing in. Finish by using a potato peeler to shave thin shards of fresh parmesan over the top of everything.

A WORD ON OUR RECIPES FOR SAUCES

In many cases, we ask you to reduce a sauce in order to intensify the flavour and improve the texture and consistency.

It goes without saying that the more you reduce, the less sauce you have at the end. Use you own judgement and taste to decide whether to add more liquid and seasoning before serving.

SEARED SCALLOPS WITH PANCETTA AND SAGE ON A POTATO CAKE

Fresh scallops taken out of their shells and served on a crisp potato cake in a dry vermouth and cream sauce.

To serve 4

16 large fresh king scallops
4 slices pancetta
a little olive oil

SAUCE
2 shallots
3½ fl oz/100ml vermouth
¼ pint/150ml chicken stock
½ pint/300ml double cream
juice of one lemon

POTATO CAKE
4 medium potatoes
2 egg yolks
1oz/25g butter
2½fl oz/75ml olive oil
8 leaves of sage
salt & freshly ground black pepper
a little flour

Preparation
Peel the potatoes and boil them in some salted water. Peel and chop the shallots and chop the sage. Remove the scallops from their shells, or if you prefer, ask your fishmonger to do this for you. Pre-heat the oven to gas mark 5/190°C.

Method
Make some smooth mashed potato by combining the boiled potatoes with the butter, olive oil, salt, pepper, sage and egg yolks. Put this on one side to cool.

The sauce is simply made by gently cooking the chopped shallots with the vermouth and chicken stock, together with lemon juice. Allow this to reduce before adding the cream and bring gently to the boil, simmering until the quantity has reduced by about a half. Remove from the heat.

Our next task is to make the potato cakes. These should be shaped into much the same size as a fish cake, rolled in the flour and fried for a few minutes each side in the olive oil until crisp and golden. While this is going on, lay the pancetta out on a baking tray and put in the top of the oven.

Finally the scallops themselves need to be cooked. These can be ruined if they are over-cooked. Therefore, the best answer is to get the pan very hot indeed and quickly fry them for one or two minutes each side. You are now ready to assemble the dish. Start by putting the potato cake on the plate and then pour over the sauce followed by the scallops and top with a slice of crisp pancetta.

SEA BREAM WITH RED WINE AND SHALLOT SAUCE

This dark shiny sauce is surprisingly delicious with bream or any good quality white fish.

To serve 4

4 skinned sea bream fillets
seasoned flour
a little oil
dill for decoration

SAUCE
3 shallots
2oz/50g butter
½pint/300ml red wine
1½fl oz/50ml balsamic vinegar
1½fl oz/50ml cassis
salt & freshly ground black pepper

Preparation
Season some flour with salt and pepper. Peel and chop the shallots.

Method
We will start by making the sauce - take a little of the butter, melt it in a pan and cook the shallots until soft. Add the red wine, balsamic vinegar, cassis, salt and pepper and bring to the boil before reducing by about half. Set to one side. Turning our attention to the fillets of bream - these should be gently coated in seasoned flour. It is essential that the oil should be brought to a high heat in the pan as this will lessen the chance of sticking. The fillets should be fried for about two minutes each side.

All that remains is to bring the sauce back up to the simmer and whisk in the remaining butter. This will give a dark shine to the sauce. Serve by first pouring a little of the sauce on to each plate and then lay the fillets on top. Decorate with the dill and serve immediately.

COD WITH A PARSLEY AND GARLIC CRUST AND SORREL SAUCE

The green crisp crust looks delicious against the white flesh of the cod.

To serve 4

4 x 5oz/125g fillets of cod

CRUST	SORREL SAUCE
1oz/25g pine kernels	**2oz/50g chopped sorrel**
2 cloves of garlic	**2 shallots**
2oz/50g parsley	**2oz/50g butter**
2fl oz/50ml olive oil	**½pint/300ml double cream**
salt & ground black pepper	**3½fl oz/100ml vermouth**
3 slices of white bread	**juice of one lemon**

Preparation
Firstly to produce the crust, make fresh breadcrumbs in a food processor. We must combine the parsley, garlic, pine kernels, olive oil, salt and pepper in a food processor and whiz into a paste. Peel and chop the shallots and slice the sorrel into thin ribbons. Pre heat the oven to gas mark 6 or 200°C.

Method
The first task is to spread the parsley paste over the cod followed by a liberal sprinkling of the breadcrumbs. Place the fish on an oiled baking tray and put in the middle of the oven. Whilst this is cooking, we can turn our attention to the sauce. Take a little of the butter and melt it in the pan cooking the shallots with the vermouth until they are soft. Add lemon juice and reduce, followed by the cream and reduce again. Complete by tipping in the chopped sorrel and finish off by whisking in the butter to produce a glossy appearance.

Once the fish is cooked, remove from the oven and place on the plates and pour round the sorrel sauce accompanied by some flat leaf parsley.

SALMON ON TAGLIOLINI WITH GINGER, GARLIC AND CORRIANDER SAUCE

Delicate slices of fresh salmon, cut diagonally and served with a sauce that is made very delicious by the presence of fresh ginger and coriander.

To serve 4

1¼lbs/550g salmon fillet
1 packet fresh tagliolini pasta
a little olive oil
salt

SAUCE
2oz/50g butter
½pint/300ml double cream
2 cloves of garlic
1 inch/25mm of fresh ginger
2 tablespoons of chopped coriander
3½fl oz/100ml of vermouth
juice of one lemon

Preparation

Peel and chop the garlic and ginger. Pre heat the oven to gas mark 6/200°C. Ideally, you should ask your fishmonger for a nice plump section from the middle of the fish as we are going to cut through the fish on the slant, producing slices that are approximately one quarter of an inch thick. For some reason, the texture of the fish is more delicate when served in this way. Put a large saucepan of water on to boil - this should have a little oil and salt added.

Method

Take a little of the butter and melt it in a pan. Tip in the garlic, ginger and lemon juice and cook until the garlic is soft. Pour in the vermouth and reduce by about half before tipping in the cream and bringing to a gentle boil. Simmer to reduce slightly and remove from the heat. The next task is to put the pasta into the boiling water and return to the heat. Whilst this is cooking, we can put the slices of salmon on an oiled baking dish and place in the middle of the oven.

All being well, the salmon and pasta will be cooked at about the same time. It only remains to bring the sauce back up to heat, whisk in the remaining butter to give a shine and tip in the coriander.

To assemble the dish, drain the pasta and arrange it on the plate. Lay the slices of fish on top and finish by pouring over the sauce.

BROCHETTE OF MONKFISH, SCALLOPS ON TAGLIATELLI WITH HOLLANDAISE

Just another wonderful way of eating some delicious fish enhanced by the presence of samphire, which gives an extra taste of the sea.

To serve 4

1lb/450g of monkfish fillet　　　　　HOLLANDAISE SAUCE
8 king scallops　　　　　　　　　　**(see page 104)**
8oz/200g of samphire
2oz/50g of butter
oil
juice of one lemon
salt & freshly ground black pepper
1 packet of fresh tagliatelli

Preparation
Slice the monkfish fillets in to one-inch chunks. Oil the skewers. Wash the samphire thoroughly at least twice. Fill a large saucepan with water adding salt and a dash of oil. Pre heat the grill.

Method
Arrange the monkfish chunks and scallops alternately on to the skewers. Season with salt, pepper and lemon juice. Add the tagliatelli to the water and bring to the boil. Whilst it is not necessary to cook the samphire, it should be warmed through in a pan with the butter. Do not add extra seasoning to this.

Make the hollandaise sauce - (see page 104) and keep warm.

When you are ready to serve the dish, place the skewers under the grill for approximately 3 minutes each side.

Serve by first draining the tagliatelli and arranging on the plate. Remove the fish from the skewers with a fork and place together with the samphire on top of the pasta. Finish by pouring over the warm hollandaise sauce.

CROUSTADE OF LOBSTER AND SPINACH WITH LEMON HERB BUTTER

Lobster taken out of its shell and served on a bed of spinach in a crisp tart.

To serve 4

SHORTCRUST PASTRY
see page 101

2 medium size lobsters
peppercorns
bayleaf
1lb/450g baby spinach
2oz/50g butter

LEMON HERB BUTTER
10oz/250g slightly salted butter
zest of two lemons
juice of one lemon
4oz/100g of mixed dill / parsley / basil
salt & freshly ground black pepper

SPECIAL EQUIPMENT
4 croustade tins 10cm x 3cm deep

Preparation
Make the shortcrust pastry as shown on page 101 and place in the fridge. Turning to the lobster, bring a large saucepan of water to boil. Add the bayleaf and some peppercorns and cooking the lobster for ten minutes - remove from the heat and allow to cool.

The last task of preparation is to make the lemon herb butter. This is simply made by putting the lemon zest, herbs and butter in to a food processor with a little bit of salt and pepper - whizzing until smooth. Roll up in greaseproof paper and store in the freezer indefinitely. Pre-heat the oven to gas mark 5 or 190°C.

Method
The first job is to make the pastry cases. Divide the raw shortcrust pastry in to four equally sized balls and roll them out to fit the croustade tins. Trim and line with baking paper before filling with baking beans. Put the croustades on a baking tray and place in the middle of the oven and cook for about 5 minutes. Remove the paper with the beans and cook for a further 3 minutes until just golden. Remove from the oven and allow to cool.

Turning our attention to the lobster, the meat must be removed from the tail and claws and roughly chopped. The baby spinach can be cooked by simply melting the butter over a medium heat and then tossing the spinach into it. This should take no more that 2 or 3 minutes. Remove the spinach from the heat.

To serve the dish, quite simply put all the lemon herb butter in to a heavy-based saucepan and melt completely without burning. Then add the lemon juice and the lobster and warm through. Place the spinach in equal parts in the bottom of each of the four tarts and arrange the lobster on the top. Finish by pouring over the remaining lemon herb butter.

FILLET OF COD WITH DEEP FRIED ANCHOVIES AND SWEET PEPPER SAUCE

This is a very striking, modern looking dish. The crisp anchovies are delicious.

To serve 4

4 x 5oz/125g cod fillets
12 tinned anchovy fillets
oil to fry

BATTER
4oz/100g flour
1 egg
¼pint/150ml of water
salt

SAUCE
3 red peppers
1 onion
½pint/300ml of white wine
2½fl oz/75ml of sherry
¼pint/150ml of double cream
salt & freshly ground black pepper

SERVE WITH
fresh watercress

Preparation
Firstly, we have to make some batter for the crisp anchovies. Mix together the egg, water and oil to a smooth liquid. Next, mix the flour and salt together and put in to a bowl, forming a well in the middle. Now pour the egg mixture in to the well, whisking all the time and continue until the entire mixture is of an even consistency. Rest this mixture for twenty minutes.

Peel and chop the onions and chop and de-seed the red peppers. Pre heat the oven to gas mark 5 or 190°C.

Method
To make the sauce, put the onions, peppers, white wine, salt and pepper in to a heavy based saucepan and cover with greaseproof paper. Put on to the heat and allow to simmer for long enough for the steam to cook the onions thoroughly. Transfer this mixture to a food processor and whiz until absolutely smooth. Now pass the mixture through a sieve and you have the base of the sauce.

Turning our attention to the anchovy fillets, these need to be dipped in to the batter and either deep fat fried (if you have the right equipment), or shallow fried - in either case cook until they are crisp and golden. Once this has been done, place the fillet of cod on an oiled baking tray and put in the middle of the oven for about 12 minutes.

Whilst this is cooking, you can finish the sauce. This is simply done by heating up the red pepper mixture and adding the sherry and cream. Bring gently to the boil and keep hot ready for serving with the fish.

The final stage is to put the achovies into a metal dish in the oven for the last two minutes of the cod's cooking time. Then place them momentarily on to some kitchen tissue to drain off any excess grease. To assemble the dish, simply position the fillet of cod on each plate. Pour over the sauce and decorate with the anchovies. Serve with watercress.

FISH STEW WITH FENNEL AND PERNOD

Pernod is the making of this dish - it tastes more elegant than it sounds.

To serve 4

8oz/200g of prepared squid	SAUCE
12 raw prawns	1 onion
3lb/1.5kg of live rope mussels	1lb/450g tomatoes
1lb/450g of white fish fillet	1 tablespoon of olive oil
2 courgettes	1 teaspoon of paprika
1 bulb of fennel	1 sprig of rosemary
8 spears of asparagus	1 bulb of fennel
½pint/300ml white wine	2 cloves of garlic
french bread	½pint/300ml of tomato juice
	¼pint/150ml white wine
	3½fl oz/100ml of pernod
	salt & freshly ground black pepper
	¼pint/150ml double cream

Preparation

The sauce takes a long time to cook for this dish. Therefore, prepare the sauce first. Peel and chop the onions, tomatoes, fennel and garlic. Place the chopped ingredients in a heavy-based pan with the olive oil and cook until the onions are soft. Then add the paprika, rosemary, tomato juice, white wine, salt and pepper and continue to cook over a low heat for about 40 minutes - it needs this long to get a good deep flavour to the stew.

Whilst this is going on, you can prepare the fish. Take the squid and chop it into one-inch thick chunks. Peel the prawns and wash the mussels thoroughly. The advantage of rope grown mussels is that they are virtually free of grit but you cannot be too careful. Skin and slice the bream in to one-inch chunks.

The courgettes should also be cut in to one-inch chunks. However, it will look more elegant if you can cut the chunks in to barrel shaped pieces, with some of the skin left on to add flavour and colour. Slice the fennel. Finally, with the asparagus, remove and keep the succulent part of this - the top 3 or 4 inches.

Method

Start by cooking the mussels in the white wine (covered in foil) for ten minutes until all the shells have opened. Discard all those where the shell has not opened. Now, remove the mussels from their shells and pass the water they were cooked in through a sieve in to a jug.

The sauce mixture should now be transferred to the food processor, taking care to first remove the rosemary. Whiz this until it is absolutely smooth and combine with the stock from the mussels. Pour in the pernod and place over a fierce heat and reduce the sauce for a few minutes. We can now tip in all the fish (except the mussels) and all the vegetables. Continue to cook gently for about 8 minutes until the fish is cooked. To finish the dish, add the mussels and the cream - stir for a minute or two and serve in bowls with hot french bread.

LAMB WITH A TAPENADE CRUST AND FENNEL AND CREAM SAUCE

Rack of lamb with a crisp savoury crust.

To serve 4

2 best ends of lamb - french trimmed and each cut in half

lamb (as above)	SAUCE
14oz/400g of pitted black olives	**2 bulbs of fennel**
2oz/50g of anchovies	**2½fl oz/75ml of pernod**
2 cloves of garlic	**¼pint/150ml of double cream**
3oz/75g of capers	**salt & freshly ground black pepper**
2 tablespoons of olive oil	**½pint/300ml of chicken stock**
4 slices of bread	
2oz/50g of parsley	

Preparation
Slice the fennel. Combine the bread and parsley in a food processor to make breadcrumbs. Pre heat the oven to gas mark 7 or 200°C.

Method
It could not be easier to make tapenade - simply put the olives, anchovies, garlic and capers in to a food processor and whiz until they form a smooth paste. Add the olive oil for another short burst on the whiz button. This mixture should now be spread over the backs of the racks before they are dunked thoroughly in to the breadcrumbs. This is now a good moment to put the lamb in to the middle of the oven on an oiled baking tray for between 15 and 25 minutes - depending on the size of the racks and how pink you like your lamb.

We can now turn our attention to making the sauce. This could not be easier - simply take a heavy-based pan and put the fennel, pernod, stock, cream, salt and pepper in together and place over a medium heat. Bring gently to the boil and simmer until the sauce is reduced down to half of its original volume. At this stage, add a dash more pernod, check the seasoning and prepare to remove the lamb from the oven. Cut each rack in to two and intertwine the bones to make a heart shape on the plate and pour the fennel sauce around it.

LAMB WITH SWEET RATATOUILLE

A classic way of eating lamb - it can equally well be eaten with rack or noisettes of lamb or a boned rolled leg. Our preference is for a rack with a crust of mustard and breadcrumbs and it is this recipe that we give below.

To serve 4

2 best ends of lamb – french trimmed and each cut in half

lamb (as above)	1 tablespoon of tomato puree
1 large aubergine	2 tablespoons of brown sugar
1 large onion	2½fl oz/75ml of balsamic vinegar
1 red and 1 green pepper	½pint/300ml of red wine
2 courgettes	1 sprig of rosemary
2 cloves of garlic	4oz/100g of breadcrumbs
2oz/50g of sultanas	dijon mustard
2 tablespoons of olive oil	salt & freshly ground black pepper

Preparation
Chop the aubergines into small pieces and sprinkle with salt. Allow to sweat for 20 minutes before rinsing and patting dry.

Chop the peppers, courgettes and garlic. Pour the olive oil in to a heavy-based pan and tip in all the chopped vegetables. Cook for 5 or 6 minutes until they begin to soften. Then add the tomato puree, brown sugar, balsamic vinegar, red wine, sprig of rosemary, salt and pepper. Continue to cook for about 40 minutes and you should have a deep red, fairly runny but very delicious sauce. Spread the backs of the racks with mustard and dunk thoroughly into the breadcrumbs. Pre-heat the oven to gas mark 6 or 200°C.

Method
Whilst the sauce is bubbling merrily in its saucepan, you can put the lamb in the oven. Depending on how rare you like your lamb and how big the best ends are, these should take between 15 and 25 minutes to cook. Serve the dish by pouring the sauce on to the plates first and then cutting the rack into two, arranging the two halves so that the bones form a heart shape.

LEG OF LAMB WITH AUBERGINE PUREE AND GARLIC AND ROSEMARY SAUCE

This is a wonderfully simple dish and there is no preparation.

To serve 4

1 leg of lamb (4lb/2kg approximately)

AUBERGINE PUREE	SAUCE
5 medium aubergines	**¼ pint/150ml stock**
3 cloves of garlic	**3 tablespoons of brown sauce**
4 tablespoons of olive oil	**(see page 103)**
¼ pint/150ml of double cream	**2 tablespoons of redcurrant jelly**
juice of one lemon	**¼ pint/150ml of red wine**
1 sprig of rosemary	**2 cloves of garlic**
salt & ground black pepper	**1 sprig of rosemary**
	balsamic vinegar
	olive oil
	salt & freshly ground black pepper

Method
Pre-heat the oven to gas mark 5 or 190°C. Place the leg in an oiled baking tin in the middle of the oven and cook for 2½ hours. This should produce lamb that is very slightly pink. You can cook for more or less time as you prefer. Whilst this is roasting, you can make the aubergine puree.

Cut the aubergines in half and cook in the oven with the olive oil, garlic, rosemary, salt and pepper under a covering of tin foil for about 40 minutes until they are quite soft. Lift the aubergines out of the baking dish and scoop the soft centres out of their skins into a food processor bowl. Discard the skins and simply tip all the remaining bits and pieces that are in the baking dish, in to the processor. Whiz the whole lot together to form a smooth paste. Finally add the lemon juice and cream and give another sharp burst on the go button. Peel and chop the garlic for the sauce.

Finally, the sauce. Heat the oil in a heavy-based pan and cook the garlic until soft with the rosemary and redcurrant jelly. Add the stock, the brown sauce, the red wine and the seasoning and reduce by half. Finish by adding a dash of balsamic vinegar to sharpen the flavour. Remove the sprig of rosemary and keep warm.

To assemble the dish, firstly warm through the aubergine puree and dollop on to the plate. Carve the joint in thick pink slices and arrange to one side of the puree. Finally, bring the sauce briefly to the boil and pour around the meat.

PAN FRIED FILLET OF PORK WITH BLACK PUDDING AND MUSTARD SAUCE

There are certain things that go with pork and certain things that don't but black pudding, apple and mustard are all wonderful.

To serve 4

1½lbs/700g of pork tenderloin
8oz/200g of black pudding
2 apples
2oz/50g butter

SAUCE
1 tablespoon of grain mustard
1 tablespoon of dijon mustard
¼ pint/150ml of stock
2½fl oz/75ml of madeira
¼ pint/150ml of double cream
a little oil
salt & freshly ground black pepper
1 clove of garlic

Preparation
Peel and slice the apples. Remove any sinew from the fillets of pork and cut in to quarter inch slices. Cut the black pudding in to quarter inch thick roundels. Peel and chop the garlic.

Method
Take the slices of pork and flatten them out a little with a rolling pin on a chopping board. Pan-fry the pork with the black pudding in the butter and only tip in the apples at the last minute when the meat is nearly cooked.

The sauce is very quickly made but is no less delicious for that. Start by heating the oil and cooking the garlic until it is soft. Then add the dijon mustard and grain mustard and cook for a few more moments before tipping in the stock and madeira. Reduce by about one third and finish by pouring in the cream and reducing a little further. Add salt and pepper as necessary and serve by pouring it around the pork and black pudding, decorating with the apples.

FILLET OF PORK WITH FRAGRANT RICE AND THAI CURRY SAUCE

This is in no way a hot curry but rather an aromatic, interesting flavoured sauce that goes beautifully with fillet of pork.

To serve 4

1½ lbs/700g of pork tenderloin
8ozs/200g of jasmine rice
¾ pint/450ml of water
a little oil

SAUCE
2 shallots
1 clove of garlic
3 teaspoons of thai curry paste
¼ pint/150ml of coconut milk
¼ pint/150ml of stock
2 lime leaves
2 teaspoons of sugar
¼ pint of double cream
a little oil
salt & freshly ground black pepper
juice of one lime

Preparation

Remove the sinew from the pork and cut in to quarter inch slices. Peel and chop the shallots and garlic. Shred the lime leaves. Wash the jasmine rice thoroughly in cold water and tip in to a heavy-based saucepan with the water.

Method

Get the rice on to cook first by bringing it quickly to the boil, then stir before simmering gently with the lid on. The trick is to leave the rice on the heat for just 10 minutes. Then remove it from the flame and allow it to cook in its own steam for a further 5 minutes and then fork through gently.

Whilst all this is going on, you can turn your attention to the pork which should be slightly flattened using a rolling pin and chopping board. This should be fried in oil in a heavy-based pan.

The curry sauce should be started in a separate pan and is made by heating the oil and cooking the shallots and garlic until soft. Then stir in the Thai curry paste and cook for a minute or so before adding the coconut milk, lime leaves, sugar, stock, cream and lime juice. Adjust the seasoning and reduce by about half.

To assemble the dish, spoon out the jasmine rice which should barely need draining as by now most of the water will have evaporated. Arrange the lightly fried slices of pork over the top and finish by spooning over the curry sauce. You can serve any number of different accompaniments with this dish, but we feel the simple sweetness of mango chutney is perfect.

DAUBE OF VENISON, PHEASANT AND PIGEON WITH HORSERADISH DUMPLINGS

To serve 4

1lb/450g of venison haunch
8 pigeon breasts
1 pheasant
2 medium onions
2oz/50g flour
¾ pint/450ml of red burgundy
2 tablespoons of redcurrant jelly
1 tablespoon of english mustard
3½fl oz/100ml of port
a little oil
salt & freshly ground black pepper

DUMPLINGS
8oz/200g of self raising flour
4oz/100g of suet
2½fl oz/75ml of hot horseradish sauce
1 dessertspoon of english mustard
3½fl oz/100ml of water
salt & freshly ground black pepper

Preparation
Peel and chop the onion. Trim and chop the haunch of venison in to one-inch cubes placing them aside in a separate container. Cut the pigeon breasts in to four quarters. Remove the breasts of the pheasant and chop in to one-inch cubes. Ignore everything else except the thighs where you should remove the bone and take off the skin, chopping the meat in to similar size cubes. Pre heat the oven to gas mark 4 or 180°C.

Method
Start by tossing the cubes of venison in to the flour and coating liberally. Then heat the oil in a heavy-based pan and fry the onions until they are soft before adding the venison. Add the red wine, redcurrant jelly, English mustard, port, salt and pepper and stir thoroughly until everything is well combined. Now transfer this mixture in to a casserole and place it with its lid on in the middle of the oven for about an hour and a half. Whilst the casserole is cooking, you can make the dumplings.

The ingredients should be divided in to two parts. The flour and the suet should be mixed well together. In a separate jug, blend the horseradish sauce, english mustard, water, salt and pepper. Then pour this horseradish mixture in to the flour mixture and mix to smooth dough. We find it is better to do this by hand than with spoons or mixers. Cover with cling film and set to one side - the dumpling mixture should be allowed to rest for at least half an hour.

Once this job is out of the way, it will be nearly time to take the casserole out of the oven and add the pigeon breasts and pheasant - adding another glass or so of port. Once you have done this, the casserole should be returned to the oven for a further 45 minutes. The dumpling dough should now be divided up in to small one and a half-inch size balls by rolling them between the palms of your hands. They should be inserted in to the casserole mixture in the final 15 minutes of cooking.

PAN FRIED GUINEA FOWL WITH GREEN PEPPERCORNS AND SHALLOTS

To serve 4

2 guinea fowl
oil
salt & freshly ground pepper

SERVE WITH
watercress

SAUCE
2 shallots
1 clove of garlic
¼ pint/150ml of stock
2½fl oz/75ml of madeira
¼ pint/150ml of creme fraiche
1 tablespoon of green peppercorns
1 dessertspoon of dijon mustard
salt & freshly ground black pepper

Preparation
Peel and chop the shallots and garlic.

Take the guinea fowl, remove the legs and discard the drumsticks that are sinewy and unpleasant to eat. Remove the thigh bone. Remove the breasts from the carcass and season them with a little salt and pepper.

Method
Fry the guinea fowl in hot oil for about eight minutes each side until the skin is turning golden. Then remove and place in the oven to keep warm. Now in the same pan, you can make the sauce. Fry the shallots and garlic in the remaining oil until they are soft, before adding the green peppercorns, stock, madeira, dijon mustard, salt and pepper. Reduce down by about one third and stir in the creme fraiche. Then reduce a little more to finish.

To assemble the dish, spoon the sauce onto warm plates and suitably arrange a thigh and breast on each plate. Decorate with watercress.

ROAST QUAIL WITH RAISIN, GRAPE AND MADEIRA SAUCE

To serve 4

8 quail
4oz/100g of chicken liver
2 shallots
1 clove of garlic
a little oil
2 tablespoons of brandy
4 slices of white bread

SAUCE
16 muscat green grapes
2oz/50g of raisins
¼ pint/150ml of stock
3 tablespoons of brown sauce
(see page 103)
3½fl oz/100ml of madeira
¼ pint/150ml of red wine
2oz/50g butter
salt & freshly ground black pepper

Preparation
Trim and chop the chicken livers, crush the garlic and chop the shallots.
Pre-heat the oven to gas mark 6 or 200°C

Method
Start by making the pate. We are only going to make a pate suitable for spreading on to the croute. For this we heat the oil and cook the shallots and garlic until they are soft. Then introduce the chicken liver and cook for a moment or two longer before flambéing with the brandy. Remove from the heat and transfer the whole mixture in to a food processor. Whiz for a minute or two until the mixture is smooth. Using the same pan, pour in a little oil heated until it is just smoking. Cut four round croutes with a 4-inch cutter from white bread. Fry on both sides until crisp and golden and place on to kitchen tissue to drain.

The time has come to put the quail in to the oven. These should be on an oiled tray and will need to cook for 15-20 minutes in the middle of the oven. Whilst these are roasting merrily away, make the sauce. This could not be simpler. Simply take a heavy-based saucepan and pour in the stock, brown sauce, madeira, red wine and raisins. Bring sharply to the boil and simmer until the sauce has been reduced by half. Season and put to one side. Put in the grapes and the butter to add shine to the sauce at the last minute.

When you are ready to serve, put the croutes momentarily back in to the oven having first spread them with a liberal coating of the pate. All that remains to be done is to place two quail on to the croute and surround with delicious green grape sauce.

RABBIT STIFATHO

A Greek peasant dish using pieces of rabbit cooked in a rich tomato sauce.

To serve 4

2-3 rabbits (depending on size)	3 tablespoons of olive oil
2 medium onions	1 tablespoon of sugar
2 red peppers	3oz/75g of stoned black olives
8oz/200g tinned tomatoes	2 large cloves of garlic
8 shallots (whole)	1 sprig of rosemary
½ pint/300ml of red wine	salt & freshly ground black pepper
3½fl oz/100ml red wine vinegar	4 slices of bread
¼ pint/150ml of water	1oz/25g of parsley
	4 slices prosciutto

Preparation

Take the rabbit, cut off the back legs and remove the meat from the bone. Cut away the fillets of meat from the saddle of the rabbit and chop in to one-inch chunks. Ignore the front legs. Peel and chop the onions. Peel, chop and de-seed the peppers. Peel and crush the garlic. Peel the shallots. Pre heat the oven to gas mark 4 or 180°C. Make breadcrumbs with fresh bread and parsley in a food processor.

Method

We start by making this dish in a large frying pan and then later transfer the whole mixture to a casserole. Introduce the oil to the pan and fry the onions, red peppers, garlic and rosemary together with the rabbit. Continue until the rabbit is completely sealed and then transfer the whole mixture to the casserole. Now you can pour in the tinned tomatoes with the black olives, shallots, red wine, sugar, water and red wine vinegar. Season with salt and pepper and stir thoroughly. Put a lid on the casserole and place in the middle of the oven. Allow to cook for two hours. When you reach the final 15 minutes of cooking, remove the lid from the casserole and spread the prosciutto followed by the breadcrumbs over the complete surface of the stifatho. Drizzle with olive oil and return to the oven to allow this topping to go crisp.

This dish can be served with salad and mashed potato made with olive oil or even grilled polenta.

RABBIT ROASTED IN PROSCIUTTO WITH BACON SAUCE

This is almost the most popular dish that we have served at the Hungry Monk in recent years.

To serve 4

2 rabbits
4 slices of prosciutto

STUFFING
1lb/450g of spinach
2 rashers of bacon
2 shallots
1oz/25g of pine kernels
2 egg yolks
2 slices of white bread
oil
salt & freshly ground black pepper

BACON SAUCE
2 rashers of bacon
2 shallots
¼ pint/150ml of stock
¼ pint/150ml of double cream
a little oil
4fl oz/120ml of sherry

Preparation
Cut the back legs from the rabbit and bone out. Remove the fillets from either side of the backbone and set aside. Discard the rest of the carcass. Peel and chop the shallots. Make breadcrumbs in a food processor. Separate the egg yolks. Toast the pine kernels. Pre heat the oven to gas mark 5 or 190°C. Thoroughly wash the spinach. Chop the bacon for the stuffing.

Method
Take a heavy-based pan; pour in the oil and place over a medium heat. Throw in the bacon together with the shallots. When these have cooked for a few minutes, toss in the spinach, salt, pepper and pine kernels and continue to fry everything until the spinach is cooked. Allow to cool, drain off any excess liquid, then add the egg yolks and breadcrumbs.

Take the boned legs and lay flat - inside uppermost. Spoon the stuffing on to them and wrap the meat around. Then wrap each leg in a slice of prosciutto and roll up. Lay the legs in a roasting dish and cook in the pre heated oven for 25 minutes.

Now is the time to make the sauce. Fry the bacon and shallots in oil in a heavy-based pan until they are cooked. Add the sherry and the stock and bring momentarily to the boil and then simmer until the sauce has reduced by one half. Pour in the cream, stir gently and set to one side. When you re-heat this sauce before serving, you should reduce it down still further (you may wish to add a little more sherry at this point). The final task is to put the fillets of rabbit in a separate oven proof dish, brush with oil and put in to the oven for the last 6 minutes of the roasting time for the legs.

The final assembly is quite simply to place the stuffed rabbit, together with the fillets (which look better if they are cut in to two or three pieces) on to a pool of the sauce.

Serve with either mashed potato made with olive oil, or even more delicious, with rosti as described in the recipe on page 86.

PAN FRIED PIGEON BREAST STUFFED WITH FOIE GRAS

Pigeon breasts stuffed with foie gras, pan fried and served on a croute.

To serve 4

8-12 pigeon breasts
(depending on size)
4oz/100g of foie gras
1oz/25g of dried cepes
4 slices of white bread
a little oil

SAUCE
2 shallots
2oz/50g of butter
a little oil
¼ pint/150ml of stock
3 tablespoons of brown sauce
¼ pint/150ml of red wine
3½fl oz/100ml of armagnac
sprig of rosemary
1 dessertspoon of redcurrant jelly
salt & freshly ground black pepper

Preparation
Soak the cepes in boiling water for 20 minutes. Peel and chop the shallots. Cut out the bread ready for the croutes using a circular 3-inch cutter.

Method
Firstly, roughly chop up the cepes. Open the tin of foie gras and combine with the chopped cepes. Season with salt and pepper. The next step is to make a deep sideways incision in to each pigeon breast and stuff as much of the foie gras mixture as you can into the space. These can now be set to one side whilst we concentrate on making the sauce. For this you need a heavy-based saucepan in to which you pour the oil. Place on a medium heat and throw in the shallots. Cook these until they are soft and then pour in half of the armagnac. Flambé and then pour in the stock, brown sauce, red wine, redcurrant jelly and rosemary. Season and continue to cook the sauce until it has been reduced by half. We are keeping the other half of the armagnac to add to the sauce at the last minute together with the butter that we shall whisk in to make a shine.

When you are ready to serve the dish, heat a large frying pan and sauté the breasts for 3 minutes each side. It is highly desirable to keep them as pink as possible, if you are to enjoy the flavour and tenderness of their meat.

Once the breasts are cooked, lift them from the pan and place in a warm place to rest. Now use the oil in the pan to fry off the croutes. These of course should be crisp and golden. Finish the sauce by adding the remaining armagnac and butter.

To serve, pour a little of the sauce on to each plate. Set the pigeon breasts down on to the croutes. Serve with a little rocket salad or watercress.

PARTRIDGE WITH BACON AND MARSALA SAUCE

To serve 4

4 partridges
8 slices of streaky bacon
½ pint/300ml of stock
3 tablespoons of brown sauce
3½fl oz/100ml of marsala

3½ fl oz/100ml of red wine
6oz/150g of bacon lardons
2oz/50g of butter
salt & freshly ground black pepper

Preparation

If you are unable to buy ready made lardons, they are easily prepared by taking a piece of unsliced streaky bacon and cutting it into ¾ inch long batons. Lay two slices of streaky bacon over the breast of each partridge. Pre heat the oven to gas mark 6 or 200°C.

Method

Place the partridges in the oven on an oiled baking tray and allow to cook for 20-25 minutes depending on the size of the birds. Whilst this is going on, you can make one of the simplest sauces in the business. Take a heavy-based saucepan and start by frying the lardons. Then add all the other ingredients except for the butter and reduce by half. The butter will be whisked in at the last minute to give a gloss to the sauce.

Hopefully, by the time the sauce is cooked, the partridges will be ready. All that remains is to position one partridge on each plate and decorate with a little greenery, such as watercress or rocket and pour the bacon sauce over each bird. If you feel there is too much bacon, you can always remove the streaky bacon from the breasts of the birds - a matter of taste.

CHICKEN NORMANDE

Corn fed chicken served in apple and calvados sauce in a shortcrust pastry tart.

To serve 4

4 corn fed chicken breasts	**2½fl oz/75ml of calvados**
shortcrust pastry	**2 apples**
¼ pint/150ml of stock	**1/4pint/150ml of double cream**
¼ pint/150ml of cider	**salt & freshly ground black pepper**
2 tablespoons of brown sauce	**sage leaves to decorate**

Preparation
Make the pastry tarts with shortcrust pastry (see recipe on page 101). Peel, core and slice the apples. Pre heat the oven to gas mark 6 or 200°C.

Method
Make the croustade tart cases (see page 102).

Roast the chicken breasts, having first brushed them liberally with the oil and seasoned them with salt and pepper. Depending on size, these should take between 20 and 25 minutes. Whilst these are roasting, make the sauce using a heavy-based saucepan. Start by pouring in the stock, brown sauce and cider and reduce by about half. Tip in the apple slices and a little of the calvados. Continue to cook for a few more minutes before adding the remaining calvados and the cream. Reduce slightly and adjust the seasoning.

At this stage, the chicken breasts should be a few minutes from being ready. This is a good opportunity to put the pastry cases in to the oven for a moment or two to warm them through – taking care not to burn them!

To assemble the dish, simply place one pastry case on each plate, carve the chicken breast in diagonal thick slices and arrange in each tart. Finish by pouring over the apple and calvados sauce. Decorate with sage leaves.

ROAST FILLET OF BEEF WITH INTENSE SAUCE AND HOT CHILLI MARMALADE

To serve 4

1½ lbs/700g of beef fillet (approximately)
a little oil

SAUCE
¼ pint/150ml of stock
2 tablespoons of brown sauce
(see page 103)
¼ pint/150ml of red wine
2½ fl oz/75ml balsamic vinegar
2 shallots
1 clove of garlic
rosemary sprig
1oz/25g of sugar
oil

MARMALADE
3 red peppers
1 onion
2 small red chillies
2 cloves of garlic
¼ pint/150ml of white wine vinegar
3 tablespoons demerara sugar
a little oil
salt & freshly ground black pepper
¼ pint/150ml of water

Preparation

We have to make the chilli marmalade well in advance of the rest of this dish. To do this, finely chop and de-seed the red peppers and the chillies. Peel and chop the onions and garlic before lightly frying with the peppers and chillies in a sauté pan (for a minute or two), until they begin to go soft. Now add the white wine, demerara sugar and water and cook lightly for a few more moments. Adjust the seasoning and cover the whole mixture with greaseproof paper. The idea of this is to lock in the steam and for this reason you should only cook over a very low heat from now on. Allow about 40 minutes for the chilli marmalade to thoroughly cook.

When you remove the greaseproof paper, check that it is not too runny - if it is, a short blast of intense heat should do the trick. You are looking for something that will be shiny and like a marmalade. Once you have achieved this, pour the mixture in to a clean warm jam jar and allow to cool, before putting in the fridge where it should safely have a life of about one month.

For the sauce, peel and chop the shallots and the garlic and chop the sprig of rosemary. Pre heat the oven to gas mark 8 or 230°C.

Method

Place the fillet on a baking dish; brush with oil and sprinkle salt and black pepper over the top. Now place in the top of the oven - we want the outside of the joint to seal quickly so that we can serve the beef rare.

As with so many of our recipes, we suggest that now is the time to make the sauce. Pour the oil in to a heavy-based saucepan and heat before tipping in the shallots, garlic and rosemary. Cook until soft and then pour in the sugar, balsamic vinegar, red wine, stock, brown sauce and continue to reduce. After a few minutes, the sauce becomes a dark rich syrup and as its name implies, it is intense!

To serve the dish, simply cut the fillet into thick slices and serve on the intense sauce. Accompanying it with the chilli marmalade and a nice dish of creamy dauphinoise potatoes.

ROAST FILLET OF BEEF WITH SALSA VERDE

This is a wonderfully simple way of eating fillet steak.

To serve 4

4 pieces of fillet of beef (6oz/150g each)
salt & freshly ground black pepper
a little oil

SALSA VERDE
3 tablespoons of parsley
1 tablespoon of mint
3 tablespoons of capers

6 tinned anchovy fillets
1 large clove of garlic
1 teaspoon of dijon mustard
juice of 1/2 a lemon
4 fl oz/120ml of olive oil
½ teaspoon of salt
freshly ground black pepper

Preparation and Method
The only task that has to be performed for cooking the beef is to make the
salsa verde. Start by tipping the parsley together with all the ingredients
(except for the oil) in to a food processor and whiz in to a smooth paste.
Now pour the olive oil, in a thin stream, through the top of the food
processor (whilst the blades are whizzing) and check the seasoning before
decanting in to a bowl. Transfer this to the fridge.

When you are ready to eat, cut the fillet steak in to four thick slices and
sauté with the oil in a hot pan so that the outside seals whilst the inside
remains rare. Test that the beef is still under-cooked by pressing down on
the middle of the steak with your finger - it should be soft and pliable like a
baby's bottom. If it has gone solid, your beef is well cooked. Finally, serve
with a dollop of salsa verde.

MEDALLIONS OF FILLET OF BEEF WITH VENISON SAUSAGES AND INTENSE SAUCE

To serve 4

1½lbs/700g approx. of fillet steak taken from the middle to narrow end
3 venison sausages
a little oil
salt & freshly ground black pepper
intense sauce (see page 65)

Preparation

Cut the medallions from the narrower end of the fillet in slices of approximately finger thickness. Cook the venison sausages in the oil and allow them to cool before slicing them on the diagonal in to slices of a similar thickness to the beef. Finally, make the intense sauce to the recipe that we give on page 65.

Method

This is a wonderfully simple and quick dish - the medallions of beef and the slices of sausage should be put in to hot oil and cooked for no more than one minute each side. Remove and arrange on the plate, before pouring around a little intense sauce. This is very good with celeriac puree or dauphinoise potatoes (see page 86).

We give below the basic recipes for cooking Norfolk and Barbary Duck that can be used in any of the subsequent recipes starting on page 71.

HOW TO ROAST DUCK THAT IS CRISP

To serve 4

2 x 3 1/2-lb oven ready norfolk ducklings
salt

Preparation
Pre heat the oven to gas mark 7 or 200°C. Prick the duck well all over and rub with the salt.

Method
Roast the ducks upside down, one inch apart in the middle of the oven for one and a half hours. After this time, take them out and allow to cool for 30 minutes. The birds will then be sufficiently cool to remove the legs and breasts from the carcasses. These should then be returned to the oven for twenty minutes on a fresh tray - skin side upward to finish the cooking and go crisp. If you are proposing to make the cassoulet recipe that follows, then do not roast the duck for the final 20 minutes at this stage. Neither should you throw away the duck fat as we will need this to give extra flavour to the beans.

HOW TO COOK PINK BREAST OF DUCK

If you are going to serve crisp duck then you can use Norfolk Duckling prepared to the recipe given previously. However, pink duck should be made using the breast of a Barbary Duck and these are generally available in good supermarkets already prepared.

We recommend that these should be sautéed rather than roasted, having first been adequately punctured with a fork or scored with a knife to let out all the fat from under the skin. There is quite a technique to doing this - put a little oil in a good heavy based sauté pan and raise the heat to a medium level. Then position the breasts fat side down having first seasoned them with salt and black pepper. Cook for about ten minutes and then turn and continue to cook for a further six minutes. Bearing in mind that we want to end up with a pink breast of duck, you must use your judgement as to when these are ready for removing from the pan. As with beef, you can tell whether the duck breast is still under-cooked by pressing down with a finger in to the middle and seeing how springy the meat is. If it has gone solid, it means the meat is over-cooked.

It is important to take the breasts out of the pan and put to one side at room temperature for about ten minutes to allow them to rest. However, there is no rest for you as you must now turn to sauce making!

CRISP DUCK ON BAKED CASSOULET BEANS

We love to eat crisp duck on this delicious peasant mixture of cannelini beans cooked with tomatoes, garlic and wine. Do not be shy about using tinned tomatoes and cannelini beans for this particular recipe.

To serve 4

2 onions	2 tablespoons of tomato puree
3 clove of garlic	½ pint/300ml of red wine
2 chorizo sausages	tabasco sauce
2 tablespoons of duck fat	salt & freshly ground black pepper
4 duck legs	3 slices of white bread
1 large tin of tomatoes	1oz/25g of parsley
1 large tin of cannelini beans	2oz/50g of fresh parmesan cheese
	2 teaspoons of herbes de provence

Preparation

Take the meat off the duck legs and roughly chop. Peel and chop the onion and garlic. Open the tins of tomatoes and cannelini beans and drain. Roughly chop the tomatoes. Make fresh breadcrumbs with bread, parsley and fresh grated parmesan cheese in a food processor. Pre heat the oven to gas mark 5 or 190°C.

Method

Take a large heavy based pan and using some of the duck fat from your earlier roasting, fry the onions and garlic until soft with the chorizo sausages. Continue to cook for a few minutes until the sausages are well on the way to being cooked and then pour in the chopped tomatoes, cannelini beans, red wine, chopped duck meat and tomato puree. Stir thoroughly and cook for another 5 minutes or so before adding some herbes de provence, salt, plenty of black pepper and a shot of tabasco.

Now transfer the whole mixture in to an earthenware oven dish and place in the middle of the oven. After 20 minutes or so, take out and arrange the duck breasts in thick slices over the top. Sprinkle the breadcrumbs over everything. Increase the heat of the oven to gas mark 7 or 220°C and continue to cook for another 15 minutes or so until the breadcrumbs are crisp.

CRISP OR PINK DUCK WITH SPICED PLUM AND BALSAMIC SAUCE

Cook your Norfolk or Barbary duck to one of the previous recipes - crisp or pink. Either is equally good served with this wonderful combination of plums and balsamic vinegar. A word of warning - this takes longer than many sauces so care will have to be taken over the timing.

To serve 4

6 plums	SAUCE
½ pint/300ml of red wine	**¼ pint/150ml stock**
3½fl oz/100ml balsamic vinegar	**3 tablespoons of brown sauce**
2oz/50g of sugar	**(see page 103)**
1 cinnamon stick	**2 tablespoons of orange juice**
4 cloves	**salt & freshly ground black pepper**
4 cardamom	**2½fl oz/75ml of red wine**
2 bay leaves	**2oz/50g of butter**

Preparation

Start by quartering and stoning the plums. Then in a heavy based saucepan, combine the red wine, balsamic vinegar, sugar, cinnamon, cloves, cardamom and bay leaves and cook until reduced by half. Tip in the plums and allow this mixture to stand for about an hour to give the plums a chance to become spiced. Separate the plums and put to one side and add the stock, brown sauce, orange juice and remaining red wine to your plum liquid. Now pass everything through a strainer. Return to the heat and reduce by about half again before checking the seasoning and tipping in the plums.

Finally, just before serving, whisk in the butter to give a gloss. Serve the sauce around the crisp breast of duck, or if you are serving pink duck, cut the breast in to half a dozen thin slices and fan on to the sauce.

CRISP OR PINK DUCK WITH RUNNY HONEY, GINGER AND THYME

As with the previous dish, this sauce goes beautifully with either type of duck but is relatively quick to make.

To serve 4

2oz/50g of fresh ginger	¼ pint/150ml of stock
3 sprigs of thyme	3 tbsps of brown sauce see page 103
juice of one lemon	2oz/50g of butter
2 tablespoons of honey	salt & freshly ground black pepper
¼ pint/150ml of red wine	oil

Preparation
Peel and chop the ginger and chop the thyme.

Method
Take a heavy based pan, pour in the oil and heat. Tip in the ginger, thyme and honey. Cook for a few minutes before pouring in the lemon juice, red wine, stock and brown sauce. Season to taste. Whisk in the butter in the final moments before serving to give a good gloss. Pour the sauce around the crisp breast of duck, or place underneath the fanned slices of pink breast of duck.

CRISP OR PINK DUCK WITH GLAZED FRUIT AND VEGETABLES AND MADEIRA SAUCE

This is one of our latest recipes and is very delicious indeed, a welcome break from many of the more routine ways of serving duck.

To serve 4

2 courgettes	2oz/50g of sugar
1 onion	3½fl oz/100ml of balsamic vinegar
2 red peppers	salt & freshly ground black pepper
1 yellow pepper	1 sprig of rosemary
grated zest of 1 orange	3½fl oz/100ml of red wine
6 plums	oil

Preparation
Make madeira sauce (see page 56). Peel and chop the onions. Finely chop the courgettes in to quarter inch slices. De-seed and finely chop the red and yellow peppers. Quarter and stone the plums.

Method
Pour the oil in to a heavy-based saucepan and tip in the onions, red peppers, yellow peppers and rosemary. Cook until soft and then tip in all the other ingredients. Continue to cook for another 15 or 20 minutes until you have something that looks like dark fruit compote.

To serve, arrange slices of duck to one side of the glazed fruit and vegetables and pour round the madeira sauce. Alternatively, if you have opted for crisp duck, cut the breast in two with one diagonal cut and lean the pieces against the little pile of glazed fruit and vegetables, giving an attractive height to the dish. Again finish by pouring around the madeira sauce.

CONFIT OF DUCK WITH SAGE AND OLIVE OIL MASHED POTATO

As so many dishes made with duck use only the breast, this is a welcome and delicious way of serving the legs - crisp and tender.

To serve 4

CONFIT
4 duck legs
1 pint/0.5l of duck fat/white flora
1 dessertspoon juniper berries
3 bay leaves
1 dessertspoon black peppercorns
1 sprig of fresh sage

MASHED POTATO
2lbs/1kg of old potatoes
3½/100ml of olive oil
2oz/50g of butter
freshly ground black pepper
salt
6 sage leaves

Preparation
The first stage is to prepare the duck legs to a point where they can be stored in the fridge. Take a large heavy-based pan and place all the confit ingredients in it. Bring very slowly to simmering point and cook for one to one and a half hours until the flavours are well infused and the duck legs are tender. Allow to cool fully. Because we only want to leave just the leg and thigh bone in place, trim and remove all other bones. If you intend to store the duck legs, place in a sterilised and warm confit jar. Re-heat the fat, pour over and seal. Place in the fridge.

Method
If you intend to serve this meal straight away, transfer the legs to an uncovered oven dish and cook for 15 minutes at gas mark 7 or 220°C until warmed through.

Now all that remains is to make the sage and olive oil mashed potato. Do this by peeling and boiling the potatoes - draining and adding the olive oil, butter, sage, salt and pepper and mashing until absolutely smooth. Serve the confit alongside the mashed potato. We don't suggest any particular sauce with this dish but feel that a very good french dressing on a green salad would serve much the same purpose. However, confit of duck would be good with any of the sauces that we give previously.

POACHED EGG AND PEA PUREE TART WITH HOLLANDAISE

A crisp individual tart filled with pea puree and a freshly poached egg topped with hollandaise.

To serve 4

shortcrust pastry	**EQUIPMENT**
1lb/0.5kg peas	**4 x 4" diameter – 1" deep**
3½fl oz/100ml of double cream	**loose bottomed flan tins**
salt & freshly ground black pepper	
8 eggs	
vinegar	
hollandaise sauce	

Preparation
There are four tasks to be performed for this dish - make the pea puree, make the tarts, make the hollandaise and poach the eggs. Leave the poaching of the eggs until last.

Method
Make four shortcrust pastry tarts - see the croustade recipe on page 101 and 102. Then boil the petit pois and whiz in the food processor with a little cream, salt and pepper. Follow this by passing the mixture through a sieve.

The hollandaise should be made in the following way (see page 104) The eggs should then be poached. At the risk of offending experienced cooks, just a word of advice on the poaching of the eggs. This should be done as follows. Pour water in to a saucepan to a level of 3 inches deep. Add a few drops of vinegar - no salt as this makes the whites go rubbery - bring to a rolling boil and crack the eggs into a teacup one at a time. Slip these gently in to the boiling water and poach for about three minutes taking care not to over-cook them as we want the yokes to remain runny.

To assemble the dish, make sure all the ingredients are warm and then spoon the puree into each tart and position the poached egg on top and cover with hollandaise.

LEEK AND POLENTA CAKE WITH OYSTER MUSHROOMS AND PESTO

One of our more brilliant inventions for our much-loved vegetarians.

To serve 4

shortcrust pastry
3 leeks
1 red onion
1 dessertspoon pink peppercorns
2oz/50g of butter
salt
freshly ground black pepper

CAKE
1oz/25g of flour
2oz/50g of polenta
3oz/75g of butter
½ pint/300ml of milk
4oz/100g of gruyere
3 eggs
salt & freshly ground black pepper

SAUCE
8oz/200g of oyster mushrooms
½ pint/300ml of double cream
2 tablespoons of pesto
2½fl oz/75ml of vegetable stock
salt
freshly ground black pepper

SPECIAL EQUIPMENT
spring ring tin
9 inch diameter x 2½ inches deep
228mm diameter x 63.5mm deep

Preparation
Make the shortcrust pastry (see page 101). Wash and chop the leeks. Skin and chop the red onions. Make the pesto (see page 103). Gently tear the oyster mushrooms in to strips. Grate the gruyere cheese. Pre heat the oven to gas mark 5 or 190°C.

Method
For this dish, you need a tin where not only the bottom comes away but the sides can also be un-clipped - generally known as a spring sided baking tin - 10-inch diameter. Line the tin with the shortcrust pastry so that the pastry comes half way up the sides. Put this in the fridge. Take a heavy-based saucepan and cook the leeks, red onions and peppercorns in the melted butter until soft. Adjust the seasoning and decant into a bowl. Put on one side.

Now to the cake. We make this by melting the butter in a heavy-bottomed saucepan and then stirring in the flour and polenta to form a roux. Now, rather similar to a white sauce, whisk in the milk to a smooth consistency. Follow by adding three quarters of the gruyere cheese. Season with salt and pepper. Allow to stand and cool slightly whilst in a separate bowl you whisk the eggs until they are thick enough to bear the impression of the whisk (if you can, use an electric whisk for this process). Fold about one quarter of the egg mixture in to the cheese sauce. We do this in order to loosen up the polenta. Finish by folding in the rest of the egg mixture.

You now have a pastry case, a leek mixture and a cake mixture. All that remains is to assemble these as follows. Spread the leek mixture over the base of the pastry case and pour the cake mixture over the top – not from too great a height as this will take some of the lightness out of the mix. Finally, sprinkle the remaining gruyere cheese over the top and whip the whole thing in to the middle of the oven. Cook for about 30 to 40 minutes in the centre of the oven until set and golden. Take care when the time comes to take the cake out of the tin - allow it to cool properly or it could well break as it is very fragile at this stage. There is no reason why you should not cook this the day before and then re-heat just before serving.

Now to the sauce. The oyster mushrooms should be sautéed with the oil in a pan and cooked until they are golden. Then add the pesto followed shortly by the cream and warm through. If at this stage things look a bit thick add a little vegetable stock.

To serve, cut the cake in to four equal slices and position on the plate with the pesto sauce poured around it. This can either be served with salad or other vegetables. It is also jolly nice cold served with a tomato and onion salad with a sprinkling of fresh basil on top.

A WILD MUSHROOM AND POTATO TART

Individual tarts with a rich filling of wild mushrooms topped with potato.

To serve 4

shortcrust pastry
12oz/300g of wild mushrooms
2 shallots
1 clove of garlic
2½fl oz/75ml of sherry
¼ pint/150ml of double cream
1oz/25g of butter
salt & freshly ground black pepper

POTATO TOPPING
5 large old potatoes
2 tablespoons of olive oil
2oz/50g of butter
2 egg yolks
3 spring onions
salt
freshly ground black pepper
2oz/50g of fresh parmesan

EQUIPMENT
4 x 4" diameter x 1" deep loose bottomed flan tins

Preparation

Make four shortcrust pastry croustades - see page 101 and 102. Peel and chop the potatoes and cook. Peel and chop the spring onions. Separate an egg and keep the yolk. Peel and chop the shallots. Peel and chop the garlic. If you are using dried wild mushrooms, wash them thoroughly and soak in boiling water for at least 30 minutes. If you are using fresh mushrooms, trim and tear as appropriate. Shave the parmesan in to wafer thin slices. Pre heat the oven to gas mark 5 or 190°C.

Method

Mash the potato with the butter and olive oil until absolutely smooth and creamy. Beat in the egg yolk followed by the chopped spring onions. Adjust the seasoning with salt and pepper. Now we move to the mushroom mixture that we prepare by first melting the butter in a heavy-based pan, then cooking the shallots and the garlic until they are soft. Next tip in the wild mushrooms - if these are the dried variety you can include a little of the fluid they have been soaking in as well. Add the sherry followed by the cream and adjust the seasoning. All this should now be cooked until the mixture is really quite thick, as we don't want it running out of the bottom of the pastry case. Allow to cool before assembling the tart.

The assembly is simple enough. Take the four tarte cases, leave them in their little flan tins as we need the additional support that these give.Spoon the mushroom mixture in equal quantities on to their bases. Follow this by piling on the spring onion and mashed potato and finish by arranging the shavings of parmesan cheese on the top. All that remains is to place them on a baking tray in the middle of the oven and cook for about half an hour until golden on top. Serve with a green salad with lashings of vinaigrette.

AUBERGINE GALETTE WITH MOZZARELLA AND PISTACHIO CRUST

Another little gem for the vegetarian - slices of fried aubergine and courgette puree on a crisp base with a fresh tomato sauce.

To serve 4

1 large aubergine
3 courgettes
2 cloves of garlic
salt
freshly ground black pepper
3 tablespoons of double cream
3 tomatoes
4 slices of white bread
a little olive oil
pesto sauce

SPECIAL EQUIPMENT
4 x 3½ inch/90mm metal rings

CRUST
3 slices of bread
2oz/50g of pistachios
3oz/75g of mozzarella cheese

SAUCE
8 tomatoes
1 onion
1 red pepper
2 tablespoons of vinegar
1oz/25g of sugar
½ pint/300ml of white wine
4 basil leaves
salt & freshly ground black pepper

Preparation
Slice and sweat the aubergines on a plate with a little salt for about half an hour. Peel and crush the garlic. Roughly chop the courgettes. Slice the tomatoes. Cut roundels of bread using a 3-inch pastry cutter. Make the pesto (see page 103). Make fresh breadcrumbs for the crust in a food processor. Shell and roughly chop the pistachios. Slice the mozzarella cheese. Pre-heat the oven to gas mark 5 or 190°C.

Method
Fry the courgettes in the olive oil with the garlic until they are soft. Transfer to a food processor and whiz until they are a smooth puree. Add the cream and some salt and pepper and whiz again. Rinse the salt from the aubergines and pat dry and fry in the same pan in which you cooked the courgettes. Lift out once they are golden and drain on a piece of kitchen tissue. Finally, fry the sliced white bread until it is crisp and again drain on kitchen tissue.

Now assemble the galette. Place the three-inch ring on a flat tray and position the crisp fried bread at the bottom. Spread with the pesto and then position a slice of aubergine followed by a layer of courgette puree. Follow this with sliced tomatoes and then repeat with more aubergine, courgette and tomato.

Finish by putting a slice of mozzarella on the top followed by a mixture of the breadcrumbs and chopped pistachios. Drizzle olive oil over the top and place in the oven (still with the metal ring around them), for about ten to fifteen minutes until golden and appetising to look at. Remove rings and serve with a surrounding pool of the fresh tomato sauce and accompany with a well-dressed green salad.

TOMATO SAUCE

Peel and roughly chop the onions De-seed and chop the red peppers. To make the sauce is simplicity itself. Put all the ingredients in to a heavy-based pan and cover with greaseproof paper. Place over a low heat and gently simmer for 25 minutes or so until everything is soft - including you. Transfer to a food processor and whiz until everything is smooth. Season to taste and pass through a sieve.

All Recipes in the Original Latin

TORTILLA OF THREE CHEESES WITH FRESH TOMATO SAUCE

Very much nicer than an ordinary omelette as the cheeses are actually melted in to the egg mixture making it rather more substantial and interesting to eat.

To serve 4

8 new potatoes
1lb/450g of baby spinach
4 x 1inch/25mm cubes of each cheese
stilton - goats cheese - brie
3 shallots
2 cloves of garlic
6 eggs
3½fl oz/100ml of double cream
salt & freshly ground black pepper
oil

TOMATO SAUCE
see page 84

Preparation

Wash and boil the new potatoes. Wash and chop the baby spinach. Peel and chop the shallots. Peel and chop the garlic. Cut the three cheeses into wedges. Make the tomato sauce (see page 84).

Method

For this dish, we need a large non-stick frying pan in to which we pour the oil. Place it on a medium heat and tip in the shallots, garlic and baby spinach. Allow it to cook until the spinach has given off all its moisture. Whilst this is going on, you can crack the eggs into a separate bowl with the cream and whisk together. Add pepper and salt. Slice the new potatoes.

Now return to the frying pan and add the new potatoes followed by more pepper and salt. Continue to cook until the potatoes are beginning to brown. Then pour over the egg mixture. Allow things to continue over a low heat whilst you scatter the three cheeses over the surface of the omelette. Continue to cook until the egg is clearly set and then flash the whole works under a hot grill until it is a nice golden brown. All that remains is to cut the tortilla into four equal slices and serve with the tomato sauce, with either an avocado salad or some watercress and French dressing.

CELERIAC PUREE AND OTHER ROOT VEGETABLE PUREES

Simply take a large heavy-based pan and put in to it a celeriac that you have previously peeled and chopped. Pour over a glass of dry white wine, a quarter of a pint of water and season with salt and black pepper. Cover with greaseproof paper and cook over a medium heat for about 25 minutes until soft. Now, move towards your food processor and with a slotted spoon, transfer the celeriac (or any other root vegetable you may be using) into the processor and whiz to a smooth consistency. Add about 4 tablespoons of double cream, stir in, adjust the seasoning and then transfer the mixture in to an open dish and serve immediately.

DAUPHINOISE POTATOES

Pre heat the oven to gas mark 4 or 180°C. Take four very large old potatoes and peel and thinly slice. In a jug, mix half a pint of cream with half a pint of milk - add one clove of crushed garlic and some pepper and salt. Arrange the sliced potato in a buttered earthenware dish and pour over the cream and milk mixture. Place a large knob of butter on the top and cover the entire surface with a generous layer of grated gruyere cheese. A final swirl of black pepper and place into the middle of the oven for about an hour and a half until the top is an appetising golden colour. It will do no harm to test the middle of the potato mixture with a skewer at the end of the first hour, as sometimes this dish can take a surprisingly long time to cook thoroughly.

ROSTI POTATOES

This dish is best prepared over two days.

Day one - Peel and steam four large potatoes for about ten minutes or until just soft. Place in the fridge overnight.

Day two - Grate the potatoes into a bowl and add one chopped onion, salt & freshly ground black pepper. Put a large heavy-based frying pan with a little oil onto the heat and put the potato into the pan. Fry until golden.

THE ORIGINAL HUNGRY MONK BANOFFI PIE

Sliced bananas and whipped cream over a thick layer of soft toffee. It is ironic that of the many dishes we have created over the years, this pudding invented and temporarily named banoffi – a cross between banana, coffee and toffee twenty years ago, has become one of the most popular puddings in the world.

It is interesting that although Nestle must have made a great deal of money selling condensed milk for this dish, they have never offered us one word of appreciation.

To serve 8-10

12oz/300g of uncooked shortcrust pastry (see page 101)
1½ tins of condensed milk (1lb/450g)
1½lbs/700g of firm bananas
1 pint/600ml of double cream
½ teaspoon of powdered instant coffee
1 dessertspoon of caster sugar
a little freshly ground coffee

Preparation
Make a shortcrust pastry flan case and bake blind (see page 101). Allow to cool.

The secret of this delicious pudding lies in the condensed milk. Immerse the cans *unopened* in a deep pan of boiling water. Cover and boil for 5 hours making sure that the pan does not boil dry - *see caution* overleaf. Remove the tins from the water and allow to cool completely before opening. Inside you will now find the soft toffee filling.

Method
Whip the cream with the instant coffee and sugar until thick and smooth. Now spread the toffee over the base of the flan. Peel and then halve the bananas lengthways and lay them on the toffee. Finally, spoon or pipe on the cream and lightly sprinkle on the freshly ground coffee.

CAUTION

It is absolutely vital to top up the pan of boiling water frequently during the cooking of the cans - 5 hours is a long time. If they are allowed to boil dry, the cans will explode causing a grave risk to life, limb and kitchen ceilings.

Hint
Banoffi is a marvellous "emergency" pudding once you have the toffee mixture in your store cupboard. We therefore suggest that you boil several extra cans at the same time, as they will keep unopened indefinitely.

WARM MINCEMEAT TART

Mincemeat topped with frangipan in a crisp pastry case.

To serve 4

shortcrust pastry	FRANGIPANE MIX
3oz/75g of sultanas	**2oz/50g of plain flour**
3oz/75g of currants	**1 teaspoon of baking powder**
2oz/50g of apricots	**4oz/100g of ground almonds**
2 apples	**4oz/100g of caster sugar**
zest of one orange	**2 eggs**
2fl oz/60ml of brandy	**2oz/50g of flaked almonds**
3oz/75g of sugar	
4 tablespoons of water	

Preparation

Pre heat the oven to gas mark 6 or 200°C. Make a shortcrust pastry flan case and bake blind (see page 101). Peel and chop the apples, zest the orange and chop the apricots.

Method

We start by mixing the brandy, water and sugar in a saucepan and bringing to the boil. Then tip in all the fruit together with the orange zest, cover with the greaseproof paper and stew gently for about half an hour. Remove the paper and check that the mixture is the consistency of a nice thick compote. If it is too runny, it should be given a further blast of the heat and stirred until the correct consistency has been achieved.

Turn your attention to the frangipane mixture that will go on top of the mix. Start by taking a bowl and soften the butter. Put in the sugar and cream until absolutely smooth and white. Then add two eggs and mix still further until fully integrated. Finally, fold in the ground almonds, baking powder and flour.

To assemble the tart, simply spread the mincemeat mixture over the bottom of the base and pour the frangipane mix over that. Finish by sprinkling the flaked almonds over the whole surface and place in a gas mark 6 oven (200°C) for about 30 minutes until golden and set. Serve warm with a dollop of creme fraiche.

FRESH PEACH AND MARZIPAN TART

To serve 4

2 ripe peaches
1 block of puff pastry
4oz/100g of marzipan
4oz/100g of apricot jam

Preparation
Halve and stone the peaches. Take the puff pastry out of the freezer and allow it to thaw. Pre heat the oven to gas mark 7 or 220°C.

Method
Sprinkle flour on your work surface and roll out the puff pastry to a thickness of about 1/8 of an inch (3mm). We need 4 circles of pastry approximately 4 inches in diameter and these should be placed on a baking tray. Place a ball of the marzipan into the middle of each piece of pastry, followed by a spoonful of apricot jam and cover this with a half of a downturned peach. With a knife, gently score around the circumference of the peach, as this will allow the puff pastry to rise around its edges.

Now transfer to the top of the oven and bake for around 15 minutes until the puff pastry has risen and looks golden and appetising.

Whilst things are taking their course in the oven, you need to be making an apricot glaze. This is done by placing some apricot jam in a small saucepan with a dash of water, stirring over a medium heat before passing through a sieve.

The final act is to remove the tarts from the oven (when they are looking crisp and golden) and remove the skins from the back of each peach. Then brush liberally with the apricot glaze.

Serve warm, dusted with icing sugar and with a tiny sprig of fresh mint.

HOT CHOCOLATE TART WITH CAREMELIZED ORANGES

A chocolate pastry tart filled with chocolate truffle prevented from killing you with its richness by the bitter sweetness of the caramelised oranges.

To serve 4

9oz/225g of flour	CAREMELISED ORANGES
3oz/75g of cocoa	**5 small thin skinned oranges**
1oz/25g of icing sugar	**6oz/150g of sugar**
2 eggs	**4fl oz/120ml of water**
1 pkt of butter	**2 tablespoons of grand marnier**
4oz/100g of chocolate	
1oz/25g of sugar	
5fl oz/150ml of double cream	

Preparation and Method

Firstly the pastry. Put the flour, cocoa, icing sugar and butter in to a food processor and whiz until you achieve a sort of breadcrumb consistency. Stop the machine, add the eggs and continue to mix until you have a ball of pastry dough. Remove from the machine, wrap in greaseproof paper and put in the fridge.

Now to the caramelised oranges. These need to be prepared and fully cooled before we can serve this tart. Firstly, place the water and the sugar in a medium sized saucepan and stir until the sugar is fully dissolved. Then bring to the boil and continue to boil until you have caramel. A word of warning - don't stir the caramel, just agitate the saucepan - take care not to go on for too long otherwise it will burn and go black. What we are looking for is a nice golden syrup. Whilst this is cooking, you should have time to prepare the oranges. If you have managed to get thin skinned small oranges, simply top and tail them and slice sideways through the fruit, producing slivers of about 1/16 of an inch thick (1.5mm). Alternatively, if you can only get thick pithy oranges, then cut all the skin and pith away and slice the fruit alone into thicker slices. Once the caramel is ready, pour in the grand marnier followed by the oranges. Allow to cool. A final word of warning - the caramel is pretty lethal stuff when it is this hot and must be treated with great care. Also you may find that if the orange slices are cold they might have the effect of setting the caramel slices around them. If this happens return the whole thing to the heat for a moment to re-melt.

We are now ready to make the chocolate truffle tart. Pre heat the oven to gas mark 5 or 190°C. Line the flan dish with chocolate pastry and bake blind to the instructions we give on page 101.

Melt the chocolate in a bowl over hot water. There is no need to for the flan case to cool - you can go straight ahead and beat the sugar and eggs together, before pouring in the cream and the melted chocolate. Now pour this mixture in to the pastry case and place in the middle of the oven to cook for 20 minutes until set.

Serve warm with plenty of the delicious caramelised oranges - these should be nice and cold from the fridge as the contrast in temperatures is pleasing.

CHOCOLATE MOCHA CREAM WITH AMARETTO

A delicious chocolate confection that is taken with a small glass of amaretto.

To serve 4

6oz/150g of dark chocolate
1 teaspoon of instant coffee
1 teaspoon of sugar
12fl oz/350ml of double cream
3 tablespoons of amaretto

macaroon or amaretti
biscuits to serve

Preparation
Melt the chocolate in a bowl over hot water. Dissolve the instant coffee in a little water with the sugar. Whip the double cream to soft peaks.

Method
Stir the instant coffee mixture in to the warm chocolate and then fold the chocolate and coffee mixture in to the whipped cream along with the amaretto. That is all there is to it. Now you are simply going to put the mixture in to little glasses and pop in to the fridge to cool. You may wish to do the altogether more complicated business of making little quenelles. In this case the mixture still has to be put in to the fridge to cool thoroughly before you attempt to make elegant little shapes with the mocha mixture. Take two dessert spoons, scooping the mixture up in one spoon, transferring it to another and then back to the first - shaping all the time. Finally releasing the mixture on to the plate with a third spoon that you have kept warm for this very purpose. However you choose to serve the mocha, the important thing is to accompany it with a glass of delicious amaretto and some sort of biscuit such as a macaroon or amaretti biscuit.

LUCY'S PUDDING

A rich chocolate mousse topped with white chocolate and decorated with kirsch cherries and cream.

To serve 4

4oz/100g of white chocolate
a little oil
chocolate mousse
8oz/200g of dark chocolate
2 egg yolks
4 egg whites
1 dessert spoons of caster sugar
1 tablespoon of tia maria
2½fl oz/75ml of double cream

SPECIAL EQUIPMENT
4 tin ring moulds (3"x1½"
or 75mm x 40mm)
TO DECORATE
cherries soaked in kirsch
double cream

Preparation
The distinctive aspect of this pudding is the thin crisp white chocolate discs that sit on top of the chocolate mouse. These need to be made first by melting the white chocolate in a bowl over a pan of boiling water. The discs are made by taking the four ring moulds, having lightly oiled them, and placing them on a flat baking tray that has first been covered with greaseproof paper. Pour in the melted chocolate to a thickness of no more than one sixteenth of an inch - the thinner and crisper these discs are, the more elegant the pudding will be. Place in the freezer for at least half an hour. Separate the eggs.

Method
To make the chocolate mouse, start by melting the dark chocolate in a bowl over a pan of boiling water. Stir in the egg yolks, tia maria and double cream. Now whisk the egg whites and as they begin to stiffen, tip in the sugar and continue to whisk until you form stiff peaks. Now whisk in half of the egg white mixture into the chocolate and fold in the other half, taking care to preserve the lightness contained in the whipped egg whites. The next move is to use the ring moulds in which we have made our white chocolate discs in for the dark chocolate mousse. Therefore, take out the white chocolate discs and return them to the freezer. Put the ring moulds back on to the baking tray that you have previously lined with greaseproof paper. You can now pour the dark chocolate mousse mixture in to the four rings to

a depth of about one-inch - transfer to the fridge and allow to set. This should take about an hour and a half.

When you are ready to serve the pudding, take the mousses out of the fridge still in their ring moulds, using a fish slice or something similar. Place one mousse in the middle of each pudding plate. Release the ring mould from the mousse by running around the edge with a knife that has been dipped in hot water. Position a white chocolate disk exactly over the top of each mousse.

This disc gives one a great opportunity to show off ones skills with a piping bag. Part of the charm of this pudding is the decoration that you can achieve on this chocolaty canvas! Generally speaking, an ordinary piping set will be too cumbersome for this task and therefore, the best answer is to make a little disposable piping bag using a triangle of greaseproof paper which has the rough dimension of 9 x 7 x 7 inches. Form the cone by laying the triangle on the table, take the right hand corner and bring up to meet the top point. Then take the left-hand corner and bring it across over the top and around behind the emerging cone shape to form a small cone approximately 3 x 2 x 2 inches. The top point is still visible and this should now be tucked inside the cone to lock everything in to place. Finally, pour a little melted chocolate into the cone and with sharp scissors, cut the point to form a fine piping hole at the bottom. It is now up to you what you design but practice first on a piece of greaseproof paper learning to gradually squeeze the hot chocolate out of the bottom.

Finally, decorate with cherries soaked in kirsch and cream. We have tried making our own cherries and kirsch but they tend to taste too raw and do not to have the depth of flavour and maturity that Griottini cherries have - these are quite exceptional - alternatively - Marks & Spencer do their own cherries in kirsch which are also pretty good.

STEAMED PEAR AND GINGER SPONGE WITH CREME ANGLAISE

To Serve 4

75g/3oz butter
75g/3oz caster sugar
125g/5oz plain flour
1 heaped teaspoon baking powder
2 eggs

75g/3oz-stem ginger
2 small pears
6 tablespoons of golden syrup
a little milk
a little butter

SPECIAL EQUIPMENT
4 x quarter pint (150ml) pudding basins with lids

Preparation
Peel and core the pears and chop into chunks. Chop up the stem ginger and mix with the golden syrup. Grease the moulds lightly with the butter.

Method
Cream together the butter and sugar. Add the eggs a little at a time, then fold in the flour and the chopped pear. If the mixture is too firm at this point, add a little milk. Divide the ginger syrup between the 4 pudding basins and top up with the pear batter. Seal the basins with the lids and cook for 40 minutes in a steamer.

CREME ANGLAISE

50g/2oz caster sugar
3 egg yolks
300ml/8fl oz milk
2 drops of vanilla essence or a vanilla pod

Start by mixing the egg yolks and caster sugar in a bowl until a pale colour. Heat the milk in a saucepan with the vanilla. Lift out the vanilla pod (if you are using one) and pour the milk on to the egg yolks and sugar, stirring with a wooden spoon. Return the whole lot to the saucepan and cook over a medium heat stirring all the time. Do not allow to boil. The penalty for not stirring is scrambled egg! Continue to cook until the custard will coat the back of your spoon in such a way that if you drag your finger across it, it will leave a clear line. Place in a jug and keep warm until served with the sponge.

KNICKERBOCKER GLORY

Knickerbocker Glory is just an opportunity to mix any combination of delicious fruit, syrups, alcohol, ice creams and sorbets in any permutation that appeals to you. The problem with Knickerbocker Glory's in so many ice cream parlours is that they are very dreary. When we first introduced them at the Hungry Monk, there were many raised eyebrows. However, we believe that ours is particularly scrumptious and the way we do it is as follows.

To serve 4

fresh soft fruit	PRALINE
(raspberries, strawberries, kiwis etc)	**4oz/100g of hazelnut**
raspberry puree	**4oz/100g of almonds**
vanilla ice cream	**1/8 pint/60ml of water**
cherry brandy ice cream	**8oz/200g of sugar**
banoffi toffee	TO DECORATE
double cream	**flaked almonds**
apricot sorbet	**icing sugar**
	cherries
	mint

Preparation
To make raspberry puree. Take good fresh raspberries and stew them in a little bit of water and some sugar. Puree them in a food processor and pass them through a strainer. To make praline by take some hazelnuts and almonds and bake them in the middle of a gas mark three oven (170°C) for 15 or 20 minutes until golden. At the same time, boil some sugar and water together until they caramelise and go a deep golden colour. Pour the caramel over the nuts on an oiled marble slab or baking tray and allow to crack hard. Pound to a granular consistency. Praline stores in an airtight jar indefinitely. To make banoffi toffee, boil a tin of condensed milk as described in the Banoffi Pie recipe (on page 87). Toast some flaked almonds. Whip the double cream into soft peaks.

Method
The drawback with Knickerbocker Glory is it has to be done just before serving - there is no way you can put them in the fridge or even in the freezer. Start by putting some fresh soft fruit such as strawberries,

raspberries, kiwi's etc into the bottom of a tall Knickerbocker Glory glass. Pour over a little of the raspberry puree to lubricate things and give a shot of colour. Now put a layer of vanilla ice cream followed by a dollop of Banoffi Toffee mixture. This can now be sprinkled with praline and covered with a layer of brandy ice cream. Next a little apricot sorbet and some more praline. Finish by piping on whipped cream which can be topped with Griottini cherries and flaked almonds. Dust with icing sugar and a tiny sprig of fresh mint. Watch adults become children again as they squeal with delight as you place this wonderful confection in front of them.

ICE CREAM

4 eggs
3oz/75g caster sugar
1pint/600ml of double cream

An awful lot of unnecessary mystique has been built up in people's minds about the business of making ice cream at home. Contraptions that whirl in the ice box, curious alpine looking wooden buckets with handles and so on are all unnecessary with this delightfully simple recipe which produces delicious ice cream every time without fail.

The base to which you add any flavour that you like is made by taking two bowls. In one, beat together the sugar and eggs until white and in the other whipping the cream until stiff.

Now simply combine the two adding the flavours and pour into a polythene box and freeze for 24 hours.

Prune and Armagnac Ice Cream

A basic ice cream recipe as above with the addition of 5oz/125g of stoned prunes, four tablespoons of water, 2oz/50g of sugar and 2½fl oz/75ml of Armagnac.

Boil the water and sugar together to form a syrup. Tip in the prunes and continue to cook until they have doubled in size. Allow to cool and stir in the armagnac. Now transfer to the fridge and leave overnight. In the morning, simply remove the stones from the prunes and chop the fruit up into small chunks. This mixture together with two tablespoons of the syrup can now be stirred into your base ice cream mixture just before you put it in to its polythene box and into the freezer.

Cherry Brandy Ice Cream

To make cherry brandy ice cream is very easy. Simply take a jar of best quality black cherry jam and whisk the contents into the base ice cream together with 2½fl oz/75ml of cherry brandy. Place in a polythene box in the freezer.

Vanilla Ice Cream

You have a number of choices here. You can either use vanilla sugar in the making of the base ice cream in place of ordinary sugar or you can add the contents of one vanilla pod to the base ice cream (seeds and all). With this latter method, you should also add two or three drops of best quality vanilla essence - not the cheap and horrible stuff that is readily available in most supermarkets.

SHORTCRUST PASTRY

6oz/150g of plain flour
4oz/100g of butter
1 egg
pinch of salt

This is best made in a food processor. Start by combining the flour, salt and the butter and whizzing in the machine until they are the consistency of breadcrumbs. Add the egg and whiz again until everything is combined. We should have something looking very like raw pastry! Place in the fridge to rest for 20 minutes before you roll it.

BAKING A FLAN CASE BLIND
(Using a 10 inch flan dish).

Make the shortcrust pastry to the recipe given above. Sprinkle flour on your work surface and roll out the pastry to the thickness of approximately 1/8 of an inch (3mm). Now pick the pastry up by rolling it back over the rolling pin towards you and carry the pastry to the waiting flan tin. Gently lower the pastry over the flan dish and push into the corners until the dish is completely lined. Finish by passing the rolling pin over the rim of the dish so that all surplus pastry falls away.

You should now prick the base all over with a fork and line with greaseproof paper. Fill with the baking beans and put the whole thing in the oven at gas mark 6 (200°C) for about 15 minutes, before lifting out of the oven and removing the greaseproof paper, with it's cargo of baking beans. Now return the flan dish to the oven for another 5 minutes to allow the base to crisp. Allow to cool.

A note on storage:
If you are going to put this in the fridge, cover it in cling film so that it stays crisp. Alternatively, you can freeze the flan in its raw state very successfully and then bake it just before you need it.

BAKING A CROUSTADE CASE
(Using 4 flan tins - 4 inches x 1½ inches)

Make the shortcrust pastry to the recipe given on the previous page. Divide the raw shortcrust pastry into four equally sized balls and roll them out on a floured surface to a thickness of about 1/8-inch (3mm). Gently lower the pastry into the croustade tins and push gently into the base. Trim the excess pastry from around the rim. Line with baking paper before filling with baking beans. Place all four on a baking tray and put into the middle of a preheated oven at gas mark 6 (200°C) to cook for about 8 minutes. Remove the paper with the beans and cook for about another 3 minutes until just golden. Allow to cool.

BROWN SAUCE

Ingredients for 2 pints/1.2 litres

3oz/75g good dripping
1 carrot
1 onion
1 stick of celery
mushroom stalks
2 rashers of streaky bacon
3oz/75g of plain flour

2 tbsps of tomato puree
1 tbsp of worcester sauce
1 bay leaf
a bouquet garni
2½ pints/1.5 litres of stock
salt & freshly ground black pepper

Preparation
Peel and finely dice the onion and carrot. Finely slice the celery and bacon.

Method
Melt the dripping in a large saucepan and fry the onion, carrot, celery, mushroom stalks and bacon until golden brown. Then tip in the flour and continue to cook for 2 or 3 minutes, stirring briskly. Gradually pour in the stock, together with the rest of the ingredients. Bring to the boil and simmer for 10 minutes. Season. Reduce the sauce by simmering, uncovered for about 30 minutes. Strain in to a jug ready for use or cool and freeze in ice cube trays to be used as required.

PESTO

2oz/50g fresh basil
2oz/50g pine nuts
1oz/25g dried parmesan
3 cloves of garlic
3½ fl oz/100ml olive oil
salt and freshly ground black pepper

Method
Place all the ingredients except the olive oil in a food processor and whiz to the consistency of fine breadcrumbs. With the machine still running, gently pour in the olive oil. The pesto should turn in to a smooth green paste that can either be used immediately or stored in the fridge.

HOLLANDAISE SAUCE

To make ½ pint/300ml

8oz/200g salted butter
the juice of 2 lemons
3 egg yolks
half a teaspoonful of dijon mustard

Method
This is a simple method of making a light creamy hollandaise using lemon juice and mustard rather than the more traditional reduction of vinegar with a bay leaf.

Start by thoroughly melting the butter, taking care not to brown it at all. Next combine the egg yolks lemon juice and mustard in the top half of a double saucepan away from the heat. Then place over the heat and whisk until thick and smooth (not scrambled!)

Transfer this to a mixing bowl ready for the melted butter to be poured in a thin stream, whisking all the time. The finished article should be smooth, creamy and shining with no sign of separation. There should be no need for further seasoning. Set aside keeping the sauce at kitchen temperature. Serve as soon as possible.

If the sauce should separate – do not be dismayed! Simply return the mixture to the heat in a double saucepan and bring up to a temperature hotter than blood heat but less than boiling. Take a clean bowl and fill it with boiling water – this warms the bowl. Pour off the hot water leaving a teaspoonful in the bottom. Now simply pour the separated hollandaise in a very fine stream on to the water whisking continuously. There are other methods of retrieving hollandaise but this way is fool proof.

To reheat leftover sauce – follow the instructions above.

Printed in Great Britain by
St Edmundsbury Press Ltd, Bury St Edmunds, Suffolk